Form Your Own Corporation

(+CD-ROM)

Form Your Own Corporation

(+CD-ROM)

Fifth Edition

W. Kelsea Eckert
Arthur Sartorius, III
Mark Warda

Attorneys at Law

SPHINX® PUBLISHING

AN IMPRINT OF SOURCEBOOKS, INC.®
NAPERVILLE, ILLINOIS
www.SphinxLegal.com

Fifth Edition: 2006
Second Printing: June, 2006

Published by: **Sphinx® Publishing, An Imprint of Sourcebooks, Inc.®**

Naperville Office
P.O. Box 4410
Naperville, Illinois 60567-4410
630-961-3900
Fax: 630-961-2168
www.sourcebooks.com
www.SphinxLegal.com

This publication is designed to provide accurate and authoritative information in regard to the subject matter covered. It is sold with the understanding that the publisher is not engaged in rendering legal, accounting, or other professional service. If legal advice or other expert assistance is required, the services of a competent professional person should be sought.

From a Declaration of Principles Jointly Adopted by a Committee of the American Bar Association and a Committee of Publishers and Associations

This product is not a substitute for legal advice.

Disclaimer required by Texas statutes.

Library of Congress Cataloging-in-Publication Data
Eckert, W. Kelsea.
  Form your own corporation (+CD-ROM)/ by W. Kelsea Eckert, Arthur Sartorius, III, and Mark Warda.-- 5th ed.
       p. cm.
  Rev. ed. of: How to form your own corporation. 4th ed. 2003.
  Includes index.
  ISBN-10 1-57248-516-7 (alk. paper)
  ISBN-13 978-1-57248-516-7
 1. Corporation law--United States--Popular works. 2. Corporation law--United States--Forms. I. Sartorius, Arthur G. II. Warda, Mark. III. Eckert, W. Kelsea. How to form your own corporation. IV. Title.

KF1414.6.E29 2006
346.73'066--dc22
                                                 2005014619

Printed and bound in the United States of America.
SB — 10 9 8 7 6 5 4 3 2

Contents

How to Use the CD-ROM

Thank you for purchasing *Form Your Own Corporation*. In this book, we have worked hard to compile exactly what you need to easily and quickly prepare the material necessary to form a corporation. To make this material even more useful, we have included every document in the book on the CD-ROM that is attached to the inside back cover of the book. Additionally, state-specific forms that do not appear in the book are included on the CD-ROM. Check the "00 CD-ROM Contents" file on the disc to see which forms have been included for your state.

You can use these forms just as you would the forms in the book. Print them out, fill them in, and use them however you need. You can also fill in the forms directly on your computer. Just identify the form you need, open it, click on the space where the information should go, and input your information. Customize each form for your particular needs. Use them over and over again.

The CD-ROM is compatible with both PC and Mac operating systems. (While it should work with either operating system, we cannot guarantee that it will work with your particular system and we cannot provide technical assistance.) To use the forms on your computer, you will need to use Microsoft Word or another word processing program that can read Word files. The CD-ROM does not contain any such program. You will also need to use Adobe Reader for the state-specific forms. The CD-ROM does not contain this program. You can download this program from Adobe's website at **www.adobe.com**. Click on the "Get Adobe Reader" icon to begin the download process and follow the instructions.

Insert the CD-ROM into your computer. Double-click on the icon representing the disc on your desktop or go through your hard drive to identify the drive that contains the disc and click on it.

Once opened, you will see the files contained on the CD-ROM listed as "Form #: [Form Title]." Open the file you need through the appropriate program. You may print the form to fill it out manually at this point, or you can click on the appropriate line to fill it in using your computer.

Any time you see bracketed information [ ] on the form, you can click on it and delete the bracketed information from your final form. This information is only a reference guide to assist you in filling in the forms and should be removed from your final version. Once all of your information is filled in, you can print your filled-in form.

•   •   •   •   •

Purchasers of this book are granted a license to use the forms contained in it for their own personal use. By purchasing this book, you have also purchased a limited license to use all forms on the accompanying CD-ROM. The license limits you to personal use only and all other copyright laws must be adhered to. No claim of copyright is made in any government form reproduced in the book or on the CD-ROM. You are free to modify the forms and tailor them to your specific situation.

The author and publisher have attempted to provide the most current and up-to-date information available. However, the courts, Congress, and your state's legislatures review, modify, and change laws on an ongoing basis, as well as create new laws from time to time. Due to the very nature of the information and the continual changes in our legal system, to be sure that you have the current and best information for your situation, you should consult a local attorney or research the current laws yourself.

This publication is designed to provide accurate and authoritative information in regard to the subject matter covered. It is sold with the understanding that the publisher is not engaged in rendering legal, accounting, or other professional service. If legal advice or other expert assistance is required, the services of a competent professional person should be sought.

> —*From a Declaration of Principles Jointly Adopted by a Committee of the American Bar Association and a Committee of Publishers and Associations*

This product is not a substitute for legal advice.

> —*Disclaimer required by Texas statutes*

Using Self-Help Law Books

Before using a self-help law book, you should realize the advantages and disadvantages of doing your own legal work and understand the challenges and diligence that this requires.

The Growing Trend

Rest assured that you will not be the first or only person handling your own legal matter. For example, in some states, more than 75% of the people in divorces and other cases represent themselves. Because of the high cost of legal services, this is a major trend, and many courts are struggling to make it easier for people to represent themselves. However, some courts are not happy with people who do not use attorneys and refuse to help them in any way. For some, the attitude is, "Go to the law library and figure it out for yourself."

We write and publish self-help law books to give people an alternative to the often complicated and confusing legal books found in most law libraries. We have made the explanations of the law as simple and easy to understand as possible. Of course, unlike an attorney advising an individual client, we cannot cover every conceivable possibility.

Cost/Value Analysis

Whenever you shop for a product or service, you are faced with various levels of quality and price. In deciding what product or service to buy, you make a cost/value analysis on the basis of your willingness to pay and the quality you desire.

When buying a car, you decide whether you want transportation, comfort, status, or sex appeal. Accordingly, you decide among choices such as a Neon, a Lincoln, a Rolls Royce, or a Porsche. Before making a decision, you usually weigh the merits of each option against the cost.

When you get a headache, you can take a pain reliever (such as aspirin) or visit a medical specialist for a neurological examination. Given this choice, most people, of course, take a pain reliever, since it costs only pennies; whereas a medical examination costs hundreds of dollars and takes a lot of time. This is usually a logical choice because it is rare to need anything more than a pain reliever for a headache. But in some cases, a headache may indicate a brain tumor, and failing to see a specialist right away can result in complications. Should everyone with a headache go to a specialist? Of course not, but people treating their own illnesses must realize that they are betting on the basis of their cost/value analysis of the situation. They are taking the most logical option.

The same cost/value analysis must be made when deciding to do one's own legal work. Many legal situations are very straightforward, requiring a simple form and no complicated analysis. Anyone with a little intelligence and a book of instructions can handle the matter without outside help.

But there is always the chance that complications are involved that only an attorney would notice. To simplify the law into a book like this, several legal cases often must be condensed into a single sentence or paragraph. Otherwise, the book would be several hundred pages long and too complicated for most people. However, this simplification necessarily leaves out many details and nuances that would apply to special or unusual situations. Also, there are many ways to interpret most legal questions. Your case may come before a judge who disagrees with the analysis of our authors.

Therefore, in deciding to use a self-help law book and to do your own legal work, you must realize that you are making a cost/value analysis. You have decided that the money you will save in doing it yourself outweighs the chance that your case will not turn out to your satisfaction. Most people handling their own simple legal matters never have a problem, but occasionally people find that it ended up costing them more to have an attorney straighten out the situation than it would have if they had hired an attorney in the beginning. Keep this in mind while handling your case, and be sure to consult an attorney if you feel you might need further guidance.

Local Rules   The next thing to remember is that a book which covers the law for the entire nation, or even for an entire state, cannot possibly include every procedural difference of every jurisdiction. Whenever possible, we provide the exact form needed; however, in some areas, each county, or even each judge, may require unique forms and procedures. In our state books, our forms usually cover the majority of counties in the state or provide examples of the type of form that will be required. In our national books, our forms are sometimes even more general in nature but are designed to give a good idea of the type of form that will be needed in most locations. Nonetheless, keep in mind that your state, county, or judge may have a requirement, or use a form, that is not included in this book.

You should not necessarily expect to be able to get all of the information and resources you need solely from within the pages of this book. This book will serve as your guide, giving you specific information whenever possible and helping you to find out what else you will need to know. This is just like if you decided to build your own backyard deck. You might purchase a book on how to build decks. However, such a book would not include the building codes and permit requirements of every city, town, county, and township in the nation; nor would it include the lumber, nails, saws, hammers, and other materials and tools you would need to actually build the deck. You would use the book as your guide, and then do some work and research involving such matters as whether you need a permit of some kind, what type and grade of wood is available in your area, whether to use hand tools or power tools, and how to use those tools.

Before using the forms in a book like this, you should check with your court clerk to see if there are any local rules of which you should be aware or local forms you will need to use. Often, such forms will require the same information as the forms in the book but are merely laid out differently or use slightly different language. They will sometimes require additional information.

Besides being subject to local rules and practices, the law is subject to change at any time. The courts and the legislatures of all fifty states are constantly revising the laws. It is possible that while you are reading this book, some aspect of the law is being changed.

In most cases, the change will be of minimal significance. A form will be redesigned, additional information will be required, or a waiting period will be extended. As a result, you might need to revise a form, file an extra form, or wait out a longer time period. These types of changes will not usually affect the outcome of your case. On the other hand, sometimes a major part of the law is changed, the entire law in a particular area is rewritten, or a case that was the basis of a central legal point is overruled. In such instances, your entire ability to pursue your case may be impaired.

Introduction

Each year, hundreds of thousands of corporations are registered in this country, and it is not a coincidence that the largest businesses in the world are corporations. The corporation is the preferred method of doing business for most people because it offers many advantages over partnerships and sole proprietorships.

The main reason people incorporate is to avoid personal liability. While sole proprietors and partners have all of their personal assets at risk, corporate shareholders risk only what they paid for their stock. With so many people ready to sue for any reason (or for no reason), the corporation is one of the few inexpensive protections left.

Creating a simple corporation is very easy. It is the purpose of this book to explain, in simple language, how you can do it yourself. A simple corporation, as used in this book, is one in which there are five or fewer shareholders, and all of them are active in the business. If you plan to sell stock to someone who is not active in the business, or to have six or more shareholders, you should seek the advice of an attorney. However, some guidance is provided throughout this book as to what some of the concerns will be in these circumstances.

If your situation is in any way complicated or involves factors not mentioned in this book, you should seek the advice of an attorney practicing corporate law. The cost of a short consultation can be a lot cheaper than the consequences of violating the law.

If you plan to sell stock to outside investors, you should consult with a lawyer who specializes in securities laws. Selling a few thousand shares of stock to friends and neighbors may sound like an easy way to raise capital for your business, but it is not. After the stock market crash of the 1930s, both the federal government and the states passed laws regulating the sale of securities. There are harsh criminal penalties for violators and the laws do not have many loopholes. The basic rules are explained in Chapter 5.

This book also explains the basics of corporate taxation, but you should consult a tax guide or an accountant before deciding what is best for you. Starting with an efficient system of bookkeeping can save you both time and money.

Good luck with your new business.

What a Corporation Is

A *corporation* is a legal *person* that can be created under state law. As a person, a corporation has certain rights and obligations, including the right to do business in its own name and the obligation to pay taxes. Some laws use the words "natural persons." A *natural person* refers only to human beings. A corporation can only be referred to as a "person" under the law, and is never referred to as a "natural person."

Business corporations were invented hundreds of years ago to promote risky ventures, such as voyages to explore the new world. Prior to the use of corporations, if a venture failed, persons who invested in it faced the possibility of unlimited liability. By using a corporation, many people were able to invest fixed sums of money for a new venture, and if the venture made money, they shared the profits. If the venture failed, the most they could lose was their initial investment.

The reasons for having a corporation are the same today. Corporations allow investors to put up money for new ventures without the risk of further liability. While our legal system is making people liable in more and more situations, the corporation remains one of the few shields from liability that has not yet been abandoned.

Before forming a corporation, you should be familiar with some common corporate terms that are used in the text.

ARTICLES OF INCORPORATION

The *Articles of Incorporation* (in some states referred to as the *Charter* or the *Certificate of Incorporation*) is the document that is filed with the appropriate state agency to start the corporation. In all but twelve states, this agency is the Secretary of State. In other states, it may be called the Department of State, the Division of Corporations, or some similar name. Appendix A will tell you what name is used in your state. For simplicity, the phrase "Secretary of State" will be used to designate this agency.

In most cases, the Articles of Incorporation legally needs to contain only five basic statements. Some corporations have lengthy Articles of Incorporation, but this just makes it harder to make changes in the corporate structure. It is usually better to keep the Articles short and put the details in the bylaws. (See Appendix B for **ARTICLES OF INCORPORATION**.)

SHAREHOLDER

A *shareholder* is a person who owns stock in a corporation. In most small corporations, the shareholders act as the officers and directors, but most shareholders do not have these roles in large corporations. Sometimes small corporations have shareholders who are not officers, such as when the stock is in one spouse's name and the other spouse runs the business. Specific laws regarding issuance of shares and shareholders' rights vary from state to state, and are listed in the various state statutes. Shareholders must meet once a year to elect directors and make other major decisions for the corporation.

BOARD OF DIRECTORS

The *board of directors* is the controlling body of a corporation that makes major corporate decisions and elects the officers. It usually meets just once a year. In most states, a corporation can have one director (who can also hold all offices and own all the stock). In a small corporation, the board members are usually also officers.

OFFICERS

Officers of a corporation usually include a president, secretary, treasurer, and vice president. These persons typically run the day-to-day affairs of the business. They are elected each year by the board of directors. In most states, one person can hold all of the offices of a corporation. (see Appendix A.)

REGISTERED AGENT

The *registered agent* (in some states referred to as the *resident agent*) is the person designated by the corporation to receive legal papers that may be served on the corporation. The registered agent should be regularly available at the *registered office* of the corporation. The registered office can be the corporate office, the office of the corporation's attorney, or the office of the registered agent.

In most states, the person accepting the position as registered agent must sign a statement that he or she understands the duties and responsibilities of the position. These duties and responsibilities are spelled out in the state statutes listed in Appendix A.

BYLAWS

BYLAWS are the rules governing the structure and operation of the corporation. (see form 5, p.187.) Typically, the bylaws will set out rules for the board of directors, officers, and shareholders, and will explain corporate formalities.

Deciding to
Incorporate

Before forming a corporation, a business owner or prospective business owner should become familiar with the advantages and disadvantages of incorporating.

ADVANTAGES

The following are some of the advantages that a corporation has over other forms of businesses, such as sole proprietorships and partnerships.

Limited Liability

The main reason for forming a corporation is to limit the liability of the owners. In a *sole proprietorship* or *partnership*, the owners are personally liable for the debts and liabilities of the business, and in many instances, creditors can go after their personal assets to collect business debts. If a corporation is formed and operated properly, the owners can be protected from all such liability.

Example:

If several people are in partnership and one of them makes many extravagant purchases in the name of the partnership, the other partners may be held liable for the full amount of all such purchases. The creditors may be able to take the bank accounts, cars, real estate, and other property of any partner to pay the debts of the partnership. If only one partner has money, he or she may have to pay all of the debts run up by all the other partners.

When doing business as a corporation, the corporation may go bankrupt and the shareholders may lose their initial investment, but the creditors cannot touch the personal assets of the owners.

Example:

If a person owns a taxi business as a sole proprietor and one of the drivers cause a terrible accident, the owner can be held liable for the full amount of the damages. If the taxi driver was on drugs and killed several people, and the damages amount to millions of dollars more than the insurance coverage, the owner may lose everything he or she owns. On the other hand, if the business is formed as a corporation, only the corporation would be liable, and if there was not enough money, the stockholders still could not be touched personally.

An example that carried this to the extreme follows.

Example:

There was once a business owner who had hundreds of taxis. He put one or two in each of hundreds of different corporations that he owned. Each corporation only had minimal insurance and when one taxi was involved in an accident, the owner only lost the assets of that corporation.

– Warning –

If a corporate officer or shareholder personally does something negligent, signs a debt personally, or guarantees a corporate debt, then the corporation will not protect him or her from the consequences of his or her own act or from the debt. Corporate officers can be held liable by the IRS for payroll taxes that have not been paid, and some states (e.g., New York) hold them liable for unpaid wages.

Also, if a corporation does not follow the proper corporate formalities, it may be ignored by a court and the owner may be held personally liable. The formalities include having separate bank accounts, holding meetings, and keeping minutes. When a court ignores a corporate structure and holds the owners liable, it is called *piercing the corporate veil*.

Perpetual Existence

In all states (except Mississippi), a corporation may have a *perpetual existence*. When a sole proprietor or partner dies, the assets may go to the heirs, but the business no longer exists. If the heirs of the business owner want to continue the business in their own names, they will be considered a new business, even if they are using the assets of the old business. With a partnership, the death of one partner may result in dissolution of the business.

Example 1:

If a person dies owning a sole proprietorship, his or her spouse may want to continue the business. That person may inherit all of the assets, but will have to start a new business. This means getting new licenses and tax numbers, re-registering the name, and establishing credit from scratch. With a corporation, the business continues with all of the same licenses, bank accounts, etc.

Example 2:

If one partner dies, a partnership may be forced out of business. The surviving heirs can force the sale of their share of the assets of the partnership, even if the remaining partner needs them to continue the business. If the other partners do not have the money to buy out the heirs, the business may have to be dissolved. With a corporation, the heirs would only inherit stock. With properly drawn documents, the business could continue.

Stock

Stock is the ownership interest in the corporation. The corporation issues shares of its stock to the people or entity who will own the corporation. A corporation can have very few shares of stock or millions of shares. The shares can all represent the same rights in the corporation or there can be different classes of shares with different rights, such as common stock or preferred stock. Stock can be designated with or without *par value*, which is usually the minimum amount paid for stock.

Ease of Transferability

A corporation and all of its assets and accounts may be transferred by the simple assignment of a stock certificate. With a sole proprietorship or partnership, each of the individual assets must be transferred, and the accounts, licenses, and permits must be individually transferred.

Example:

If a sole proprietorship is sold, the new owner will have to get a new license (if one is required), set up his or her own bank account, and apply for a new federal taxpayer identification number and new state tax account numbers. The title to any vehicles and real estate will have to be put in his or her name, and all open accounts will have to be changed to his or her name. He or she will probably have to submit new credit applications. With a corporation, all of these items remain in the same corporate name.

NOTE: *In some cases, the new owners of a corporation will have to submit personal applications for things such as credit or liquor licenses.*

Control

By distributing stock, the owner of a business can share the profits of a business without giving up control.

Example:

If John wants to give his children some of the profits of his business, he can give them stock and pay dividends to them without giving away any management control. This would not be possible with a partnership or sole proprietorship.

Raising Capital

A corporation may raise capital by selling stock or borrowing money. A corporation does not pay taxes on money it raises by the sale of stock.

Example:

If a corporation wants to expand, the owners can sell off 10%, 25%, or 45% of the stock and still remain in control of the business. Many individuals considering investing may be more willing to invest if they know they will have a piece of the action in the form of stock.

NOTE: *There are strict rules about the sale of stock, with criminal penalties and triple damages for violators. (see Chapter 5.)*

Separate Record Keeping

A corporation is required to keep its bank accounts and records separate from the accounts of its stockholders. A sole proprietor or partnership may mix business and personal accounts, a practice that often causes confusion in record keeping and is not recommended.

Tax Advantages

There are several tax advantages that are available only to corporations, such as:

- ✪ medical insurance for families may be fully deductible;

- ✪ tax-deferred trust can be set up for a retirement plan; and,

- ✪ losses are fully deductible for a corporation, whereas an individual must prove there was a profit motive before deducting losses.

Estate Planning   Shares of a company can be distributed more easily with a corporation than with a partnership. Heirs can be given different percentages and control can be limited to the appropriate parties.

Prestige   The name of a corporation often sounds more prestigious than the name of a sole proprietor. John Smith d/b/a Acme Builders sounds like a lone man. Acme Builders, Incorporated sounds as if it might be a large operation. It has been suggested that an individual who is president of a corporation looks more successful than one doing business in his or her own name. The appearance of a business starts with its name.

Separate Credit Rating   A corporation has its own credit rating that may be better or worse than the shareholder's personal credit rating. A corporate business can go bankrupt and the shareholder's personal credit will remain unharmed. Conversely, one shareholder's credit may be bad, but the corporation will maintain a good rating. For example, if one shareholder gets a judgment against him or her, this would usually not affect the business of the corporation, whereas it could put an end to a business that was a partnership.

DISADVANTAGES

Even though there are several advantages to incorporating your business, there are also additional requirements that must be met by the business owner, which some consider disadvantages. The following are some of these requirements.

Extra Tax Return and Annual Report   A corporation is required to file its own tax return. This is a bit longer and more complicated than the form required for a sole proprietorship or partnership. Additional expenses for the services of an accountant may be required. Typically, a corporation must also file a simple annual report with the state (which lists names and addresses of officers and directors) and pay a fee.

Separate Records   The shareholders of a corporation must be careful to keep their personal business separate from the business of the corporation. The corporation must have its own records, keep minutes of meetings, and keep all corporate money separate from personal money.

Extra Expenses

There are additional expenses in operating a corporation. People who employ an attorney to form their corporation pay a lot more than people who use this book. Also, in some states, a shareholder may have to pay unemployment or workers' compensation insurance for him- or herself, which he or she would not have to pay as a sole proprietor.

Checking Accounts

Under federal law, checks made out to a corporation cannot be cashed by a shareholder. They must be deposited into a corporate account. Some banks have higher fees just for corporations.

Legal Representation

Unlike sole proprietors or partners, who can represent themselves in court proceedings, a corporation usually must be represented by an attorney. This may not be necessary in small claims court.

CORPORATIONS COMPARED TO LLCS

Limited liability companies (LLCs) are the newest type of business entity. Like corporations, they offer many benefits over partnerships and sole proprietorships. Whether an LLC or a corporation is better for a small business depends on the type of business. The best comparison here is between an LLC and an S corporation, which is a particular kind of corporation discussed in further detail in Chapter 3.

Corporation Advantages

An S corporation has an advantage over an LLC, which is treated as a disregarded entity, in that the owners of the S corporation can take out some profits without Social Security taxes. However, an LLC can elect to be taxed as an S corporation.

For a large business in which the owners take out salaries of $87,000 or more plus profits, there would not be much difference, since the Social Security tax cuts out at about that level. However, for a smaller business, in which an owner could take out a $30,000 salary and $20,000 profit, the extra taxes on the $20,000 would be over $3,000.

If a corporation plans to go public or sell stock to a large group of people, the corporate stock might be easier to sell than membership interests in the LLC.

LLC Advantages

The most important advantage of an LLC is that in some states, creditors of the owners cannot get the assets of the LLC. With a corporation, creditors of the corporation cannot get the shareholders' assets (if done correctly), but creditors of the shareholders can get their corporate stock.

The other advantages of LLCs are found in certain tax situations. For example, an LLC can make special allocations of profits and losses among members, whereas S corporations cannot. S corporations must have one class of ownership in which profits and losses are allocated according to the percentage ownership. In an LLC, money borrowed by the company can increase the tax basis (and lower the taxes) of the owners, whereas in an S corporation, it does not. Contributing property to set up an LLC is not taxable, even for minority interest owners, whereas for a corporation, regulations only allow it to be tax-free for the contributors who have control of the business. (Internal Revenue Code (IRC), Sec. 351.)

The owners of an LLC can be foreign persons, other corporations, or any kind of trust, whereas the owners of S corporations cannot. An LLC may have an unlimited number of members, while an S corporation is limited to one hundred.

Choosing the Best Type of Corporation

Before forming a corporation, you must make a few choices. Will it be an S or a C corporation? Will it be a closely-held corporation, a professional service corporation, or a not-for-profit corporation? The choices you must make are discussed in this chapter, along with the features of the corporation types you have to choose from.

DOMESTIC CORPORATION OR FOREIGN CORPORATION

A person wishing to form a corporation must decide whether the corporation will be a *domestic corporation* or a *foreign corporation*. A domestic corporation is one formed in the state in which it is doing business. A foreign corporation is one incorporated in another state or country.

Delaware Corporations   In the past, there was some advantage to incorporating in Delaware, since that state had very liberal laws regarding corporations. Many national corporations are incorporated there. However, in recent years, most states have liberalized their corporation laws—so today, there is no advantage to incorporating in Delaware for most people.

If your state has high corporate fees (such as California), you might save some money by incorporating in Delaware if you are not actively conducting business in your state. If your state has high income taxes (i.e., New York), you might lower your taxes by having your local corporation pay out all of its profits to a Delaware corporation (which does not pay Delaware income tax if it is not doing business in Delaware).

Nevada Corporations

Nevada has liberalized its corporation laws recently to attract businesses. It allows bearer stock and has other rules that allow more privacy to corporate participants. It also does not share information with the Internal Revenue Service and does not have a state income tax.

Double Incorporation

One way that a Nevada, Delaware, or other corporation can be useful is if your state has high income taxes. By using two corporations, you could transfer your profits to a state that has no income tax.

Example:

Suppose you were a painting contractor who owned a building and equipment. You could incorporate in your home state as a painting contractor, but put the building and equipment into a Nevada corporation. The Nevada corporation would then lease these to the local corporation. After paying the workers, buying supplies, paying you a salary, and making lease payments to the Nevada corporation, your local company could break even with no taxable profit. The profit would all be in the Nevada corporation, which may not be required to pay taxes in your state.

From a federal tax standpoint there would seldom be an issue, because taxes would have to be paid on the profits no matter which corporation they were in.

From a state tax standpoint there would be a couple of issues. For example, one is whether the Nevada corporation was *doing business* in your state. If the acts of the Nevada corporation are passive enough, it might not even need to register as doing business in your state. For example, if it just loaned money to your corporation, it would not have to register (especially if you happened to go to Las Vegas to sign the loan papers). In most states, merely owning rental real estate does not require a corporation to register.

A second issue would be whether your state has any *catch-all* tax laws that would prevent this kind of setup. If you are going to set up two corporations for this purpose, you should meet with a local tax specialist to be sure that it is done correctly under your state requirements.

Additional Considerations   If you form a corporation in a state other than the one in which your business is located, you will be required to have an agent or an office in that state, and you will have to register as a foreign corporation doing business in your state. This is more expensive and more complicated than incorporating in your own state. Also, if you are sued by someone who is not in your state, he or she can sue you in the state in which you are incorporated, which would probably be more expensive for you than a suit filed in your local court. In some states, your corporation may be required to pay state income tax.

S CORPORATION OR C CORPORATION

A corporation has a choice of how it wants to be taxed. It can make the election at the beginning of its existence or at the beginning of a new tax year. The choices follow.

S Corporation   Formerly called a "Subchapter S corporation," an *S corporation* pays no income tax and may only be used for small businesses. All of the income or losses of the corporation for the year are passed through to the shareholders, who report them on their individual returns. At the end of each year, the corporation files an *information return*, listing all of its income, expenses, depreciation, etc., and sends each shareholder a notice of his or her share as determined by percentage of stock ownership.

Advantages. Using this method avoids double taxation and allows the pass-through of losses and depreciation. For tax purposes, the business is treated as a partnership. Since tax losses are common during the initial years due to start-up costs, many businesses elect

S status and switch over to C corporation status in later years. Be aware that once a corporation terminates its S status, there is a waiting period before it can switch back. Typically, S corporations do not have to pay state corporate income tax.

Disadvantages. If stockholders are in high income brackets, their share of the profits will be taxed at those rates. Shareholders who do not *materially participate* in the business cannot deduct losses. Some fringe benefits, such as health and life insurance, may not be tax deductible.

Requirements. To qualify for S corporation status, the corporation must:

- ✪ have no more than one hundred shareholders, none of whom are nonresident aliens or corporations, and all of whom consent to the election (shares owned by a husband and wife jointly are considered owned by one shareholder);

- ✪ have only one class of stock;

- ✪ not be a member of an *affiliated group* (only individuals, estates, and certain exempt organizations and trusts qualify);

- ✪ generate at least 20% of its income in this country and have no more than 20% of its income from passive sources (interest, rents, dividends, royalties, securities transactions); and,

- ✪ file **Election by a Small Business Corporation (IRS Form 2553)** with the IRS before the end of the fifteenth day of the third month of the tax year for which it is to be effective, and be approved by the IRS. (see form 10, p.203.) Approval is usually routine.

C Corporation   A *C corporation* pays taxes on its net earnings at corporate rates. Salaries of officers, directors, and employees are taxable to them and deductible to the corporation. However, money paid out in dividends is taxed twice. It is taxed at the corporation's rate as part of its profit, and then at the individual stockholders' rates as income, when distributed by the corporation to them.

Advantages. If taxpayers are in a higher tax bracket than the corporation and the money will be left in the company for expansion, taxes are saved. Fringe benefits, such as health, accident, and life insurance, are deductible expenses.

Disadvantages. Double taxation of dividends by the federal government can be a big disadvantage. Also, most states have an income tax that only applies to C corporations and applies to all income over a certain amount.

NOTE: *Neither of these taxes applies to money taken out as salaries. Many small business owners take all profits out as salaries to avoid double taxation and state income tax. However, there are rules requiring that salaries be reasonable. If a stockholder's salary is deemed to be too high relative to his or her job, the salary may be considered to be partially a dividend and subject to double taxation.*

Requirements. None.

NOTE: *All corporations are C corporations unless they specifically elect to become S corporations.*

Closely-Held Corporation

A *closely-held corporation* election is beneficial for many small businesses. Its purpose is to place restrictions on the transferability of stock. Often, it obligates a shareholder to offer to the corporation or the shareholders the opportunity to purchase the stock before offering it to any outside purchaser. If the corporation and shareholders reject the offer, they typically must still consent to who the transferee (buyer) of the shares will be.

If you elect to have these restrictions, they should be included in the bylaws, printed on the certificates, and in many states, they must be included in the Articles of Incorporation.

PROFESSIONAL CORPORATIONS

Under the laws of most states, certain types of services can only be rendered by a corporation if it is a *professional association* (P.A.) or *professional service corporation* (P.C.). These include such professionals as attorneys, physicians, certified public accountants, veterinarians, architects, life insurance agents, and chiropractors. For simplicity, these will be referred to as *professional service corporations*. A professional service corporation typically has specific rules under the state incorporation statutes.

Purpose

A professional service corporation must usually have one specific purpose spelled out in the Articles of Incorporation, and that purpose must be to practice a specific profession. It may not engage in any other business, but it may invest its funds in real estate, stocks, bonds, mortgages, or other types of investments. A professional service corporation may change its purpose to another legal purpose, but it will then no longer be a professional service corporation.

Name

In most states, the name of a professional service corporation must contain the words "chartered," "professional association," or "professional corporation," or the abbreviations "P.A." or "P.C." Typically, it may not use the words "company," "corporation," "incorporated," or any abbreviation of these. (see Appendix A.)

Shareholders

According to the law in most states, only persons licensed to practice a profession may be shareholders of a professional service corporation engaged in that practice. A shareholder who loses the right to practice must immediately sever all employment with, and financial interests in, such a corporation. If such a shareholder does not sever these ties, the corporation may be dissolved by the state. No shareholder may enter into a voting trust or other similar arrangement with anyone.

Merger

A professional service corporation may not merge with any other corporation except a professional service corporation that is licensed to perform the same type of service.

Requirements

Most states have very specific requirements for the formation of professional service corporations. They often require specific language in the Articles, charter, or bylaws. For this type of corporation, you should consult an attorney.

NONPROFIT CORPORATIONS

Nonprofit corporations are usually used for social clubs, churches, and charities, and are beyond the scope of this book. While they are similar to for-profit corporations in many aspects, such as limited liability and the required formalities, there are additional state and federal requirements that must be met.

In some cases, a business can be formed as a nonprofit corporation. It would not be allowed to distribute profits to its founders, but it could pay substantial salaries and enjoy numerous tax advantages.

Start-Up
Procedures

The steps necessary to legally establish your corporation are not difficult, but still need to be followed closely. Such preliminary things as checking on available corporate names must be done, as well as filing the required paperwork and acquiring taxpayer information. This chapter will take you through these steps.

NAME SEARCH

The first thing to do before starting a corporation is to thoroughly check out the name you wish to use to be sure it is not already being used by someone else. Many businesses have been forced to stop using their name after spending thousands of dollars promoting it.

Corporate Records
The first place to check is your Secretary of State's office to see if the name has already been used by another corporation in your state. To do this, you can write or call their office. (See Appendix A for phone numbers and addresses.) In some states, you can access your state's corporate records through the Internet and conduct your own search of all current and dissolved corporations. Websites are also included in

Appendix A. If your state's records are not listed or have changed, you may be able to access them through the following site:

www.findlaw.com/11stategov/index.html

Fictitious Names

Besides checking corporate names, you should check if another business is using the name you want as a *fictitious name*. In some states these are registered with each county and in others they are registered with the Secretary of State. Some states that register the names with the Secretary of State can be searched over the Internet as described above.

NOTE: *The fictitious name search may be separate from the corporate name search.*

Business Listings

Since some businesses neglect to properly register their name (yet still may have superior rights to the name) you should also check phone books and business directories. Many libraries have phone books from around the country as well as directories of trade names.

Yellow Page Listings

If you have a computer with Internet access, you can search every Yellow Page listing for free. Just search for "yellow pages" with any Web search engine (i.e., Google, Yahoo, WebCrawler, Lycos, etc.). You can select a state and enter your business name. It will tell you if any other companies are listed with that name. One site that allows you to search all states at once is:

www.switchboard.com

Trademark Search

To be sure that you are not violating a registered trademark, you should have a search done of the records of the *United States Patent and Trademark Office* (PTO). In the past, this required a visit to their offices or the hiring of a search firm for over a hundred dollars. The PTO put its trademark records online, so now you can now search them through the PTO website. Go to **www.uspto.gov** and click on the "Trademarks" button. Click on "Search Trademarks," which will take you to the *Trademark Electronic Search System* (TESS).

For a more thorough search, you can have the search done through a firm. The following firms conduct searches.

Government Liaison Services, Inc.
200 North Glebe Road
Suite 321
Arlington, VA 22203
800-642-6564
703-524-8200
www.trademarkinfo.com

Thomson & Thomson
500 Victory Road
North Quincy, MA 02171-3145
800-692-8833
www.thomson-thomson.com

XL Corporate Service
62 White Street
New York, NY 10013
800-529-6278
212-431-5000

Name Reservation

It is possible to reserve a name for a corporation for a certain period of time by filing a reservation form and paying the appropriate fee. (See Appendix A for your state's information.) However, this is usually pointless because it is just as easy to file the Articles as it is to reserve the name. One possible reason for reserving a name would be to hold it while waiting for a trademark name search to arrive.

Fictitious Names

Since a corporation has a legal name, it does not need a fictitious name, but corporation may operate under a fictitious or assumed name just as an individual can. This is done when a corporation wants to operate several businesses under different names or if the business name is not available as a corporate name. Fictitious names are either registered in each county or are registered statewide with the Secretary of State. However, registering a fictitious name does not give the registrant any rights to the name. While corporate names are carefully checked by the Secretary of State and disallowed if they are similar to others, in many states, fictitious names are filed without checking and any number of people may register the same name. The cost of registering a fictitious name varies. Application forms and instructions can be obtained from your local courthouse, appropriate county office, or Secretary of State's office.

NOTE: *When a fictitious name is used by a corporation, the corporate name should also be used. This is because if the public does not see that they are dealing with a corporation, they may be able to pierce the corporate veil and sue the stockholders individually. Thus, all signs, business cards, etc., should list the names in one of the following ways:*

Smith Enterprises, Inc. d/b/a Internet Resources

or

Internet Resources, a division of Smith Enterprises, Inc.

Similar Names

Sometimes it seems as if every good name is taken. However, a name can often be modified slightly or used on a different type of product or service. Try different variations if your favorite is taken. Another possibility is to give the corporation one name and then do business under a fictitious name.

Example:

If you want to use the name "Flowers by Freida" in Pensacola and there is already a "Flowers by Freida, Inc." in Miami, you might incorporate under the name "Freida Jones, Inc." and then register the corporation as doing business under the fictitious name "Flowers by Freida." Unless "Flowers by Freida, Inc." has registered a trademark for the name either in Florida or nationally, you will probably be able to use the name.

NOTE: *You should realize that you might run into complications later, especially if you decide to expand into other areas of the state or other states. One protection available would be to register the name used on your goods or services as a trademark. This would give you exclusive use of the name anywhere that it was not already being used.*

Forbidden Names

A corporation may not use certain words in its name if there would be a likelihood of confusion. There are state and federal laws that control the use of these words. In most cases, your application will be rejected if you use a forbidden word. Some of the words that may not be used in some states without special licenses or registration are:

Assurance	Disney
Bank	Insurance
Banker	Olympic
Banking	Trust
Credit Union	

If you use a word that is forbidden, your papers will most likely be returned. You may wish to call the corporate registrar to ask if the name you plan to use is allowed.

Trademarks The name of a business may not be registered as a *trademark*, but a name used on goods or to sell services may be registered, and such registration will grant the holder exclusive rights to use that name except in areas where someone else has used the name. A trademark may be registered both in your state and in the United States Patent and Trademark Office.

Each trademark is registered for a certain *class* of goods. You may usually register the name "Zapata" chewing gum even if someone has registered the name "Zapata" for use on shoes. One exception to this rule is if the name is so well known that your use would cause confusion. For example, you could not use "Coca-Cola" as a brand of shoes, because people are so familiar with the Coca-Cola company that they might think the company started a line of shoes. If you want to register the mark for several types of goods or services, you must register it for each different class into which the goods or services fall, and pay a separate fee for each category.

For protection within each state, the mark may be registered with each state's appropriate department handling trademarks. The cost varies from state to state. Application forms and instructions can be obtained through the same department.

For protection across the entire United States, the mark can be registered with the United States Patent and Trademark Office. At the time of publication of this book, the fee is $375. The procedure for federal registration is more complicated than state registration and is beyond the scope of this book. Visit the PTO website at **www.uspto.gov** for more information.

ARTICLES OF INCORPORATION

To create a corporation, a document must be filed with the state agency that keeps corporate records, which in most states is the Secretary of State. In most states, this document is called the *Articles of Incorporation*. However, in some states, it may be called the *Certificate of Incorporation*, *Articles of Association*, or the *Charter*. This document is referred to as the Articles of Incorporation throughout this book. Some corporations have long, elaborate Articles that describe numerous powers and functions, but most of this is unnecessary. The powers of corporations are explained in state law and do not have to be repeated. Short Articles are just as legal and allow more flexibility.

Typically, state law requires only a minimum amount of detail be included in the Articles of Incorporation. Some things, such as the purpose of the corporation, regulations for the operation of the corporation, and a par value of the stock, may be explained in the Articles of Incorporation. This is not advisable unless required, since any changes would necessitate the complicated process of amending the Articles. It is better to explain these terms in the bylaws. The matters typically required to be contained in the Articles and a few of the optional provisions follow.

Name of the corporation. Most states require that the corporation name contain one of the following six words:

- ✪ Incorporated

- ✪ Inc.

- ✪ Corporation

- ✪ Corp.

- ✪   Company

- ✪   Co.

(The specific name requirements for your state are listed in Appendix A.)

The reason for the requirement is so that persons dealing with the business will be on notice that it is a corporation. This is important in protecting the shareholders from liability.

Address of the corporation. The street address of the principal office and the mailing address of the corporation must be provided.

The number of shares of stock the corporation is authorized to issue. This is usually an even number, such as 100, 1,000, or 1,000,000.

In some cases it may be advantageous to issue different *classes* of stock—such as common and preferred, or voting and nonvoting—but such matters should be discussed with an attorney or accountant.

If there are different classes of stock, then the Articles of Incorporation must contain a designation of the classes and a statement of the preferences, limitations, and relative rights of each class. In addition, if there are to be any preferred or special shares issued in *series*, then the Articles must explain the relative rights and preferences, and any authority of the board of directors to establish preferences. Any preemptive rights must also be explained.

This book explains how to form a corporation with one class of stock. It is usually advisable to authorize double or quadruple the amount of stock that will be initially issued. The unissued stock can be issued later if more capital is contributed by a shareholder or by a new member of the business.

One important point to keep in mind when issuing stock relates to par value. *Par value* is the total number of shares that a corporation may issue under its Articles, divided by the total initial investment in the corporation. Par value is not always the actual value of the stock because a corporation's net worth may play a role. When issuing stock, the full par value must be paid for in shares. If this is not done, then the shareholder can later be held liable for the full par value. For more important information about issuing stock, see Chapter 5.

The name of the registered agent and the address of the registered office, along with the agent's acceptance. Each corporation must have a *registered agent* and a *registered office*. The registered office can be the business office of the corporation if the registered agent works out of that office, it can be the office of another individual who is the registered agent (such as an attorney), or it may be a corporate registered agent's office. Technically, it may not be a residence, unless that address is also a business office of the corporation. Penalty for failure to comply can be the inability to maintain a lawsuit and a possible fine.

The name and address of the incorporator of the corporation. This may be any person, even if that person has no future interest in the corporation. There are companies in state capitals that will, on a moment's notice, have someone run over to the Secretary of State to file corporate Articles that are later assigned to the real parties in interest. However, in some states, those who maintain deposits of funds with the Secretary of State are allowed to file Articles by facsimile, so there is less need to run these days.

Duration. In most states, the duration of the corporation need not be mentioned if it is to be *perpetual*. If not, the duration must be specified in the Articles.

Effective date. A specific effective date may be in the Articles, but is not required. Articles are effective upon filing. If an effective date is specified, state law varies as to the time before or after the filing in which the Articles of Incorporation are effective.

Execution   The Articles of Incorporation must be signed by the incorporator and dated. Typically, the registered agent must sign a statement accepting his or her duties as such. This is sometimes done as a separate form or sometimes on the same form as the Articles.

Forms The Articles of Incorporation need not be on any certain form. They can be typed on blank paper or can be on a fill-in-the-blank form. **ARTICLES OF INCORPORATION** template forms for each state are located in Appendix B. Some states have their own incorporation forms, which you can get by mail or over the Internet. (The addresses, phone numbers, and Internet addresses for each state are in Appendix A.)

NOTE: *On the accompanying CD-ROM, blank, state-specific forms that can be filled in are available from each state that provides a form. It is best to use the state form when available, but in most places, it is not required. Check to see if your state's form is available on the CD-ROM or your state's website.*

The Articles of Incorporation must be filed with the Secretary of State by sending them to the address listed in Appendix A, along with the filing fees. The fees (as available at time of publication) are listed in Appendix A as well. If you wish to receive a certified copy of the Articles, the cost is additional. In many states this is an unnecessary expense, since a certified copy is rarely, if ever, needed. Ask your bank if it will require a certified copy. Usually, the better alternative is to enclose a photocopy along with the Articles and ask that it be stamped with the filing date and returned. Appendix C has a **LETTER TO SECRETARY OF STATE**. (see form 1, p.171.)

In most states, the return time for the Articles is usually a week or two. If there is a need to have them back quickly, you might be able to send them and have them returned by a courier such as Federal Express, Airborne Express, or UPS with prepaid return. Call your Secretary of State for details.

SHAREHOLDER AGREEMENT

When there are two or more shareholders in a corporation, they should consider drawing up a shareholder agreement. This document explains what is to happen in the event of a disagreement between the parties. In closely-held corporations, the minority shareholders have a risk of being locked into a long-term enterprise with little or no way to withdraw their capital. Even family corporations should consider a *shareholder agreement*, since it could settle some issues without the expense of litigation.

A shareholder agreement is a fairly complicated document and should be drawn up by an attorney. This may be costly, but the expense should be weighed against the costs of lengthy litigation should the parties break up.

Some of the issues that are usually included in a **SHAREHOLDER AGREEMENT** are discussed below, and a simple **SHAREHOLDER AGREEMENT** form is included in Appendix C. (see form 24, p.249.) This might suit your needs while your corporation is small. Be sure to review it as your company grows to be sure it still fits your needs.

When drawing up a Shareholder Agreement, you will consider your options during the expansion of your company, but be sure to also consider the possibility of negative events, such as bankruptcy or death of a participant. These are the times when a Shareholder Agreement is most needed.

Rights of Minority

The biggest risk in a small corporation with unequal ownership is that an owner of a minority interest will be shut out of making decisions. Unless some rights are spelled out in a Shareholder Agreement, any shareholder with less than 50% interest risks having his or her investment tied up indefinitely. Many of the clauses in a Shareholder Agreement address various rights (such as salary and withdrawal) of shareholders with a minority interest.

Supermajority Vote or Unanimous Consent

In order to allow shareholders with minority interests to have a say in major changes in the corporation, you can require unanimous consent or more than simple majority vote (*supermajority*) on such issues. One danger to keep in mind is that requiring unanimous consent can allow one disgruntled shareholder to sabotage the efforts of the majority.

Example:
If the majority wants to sell the company, you would not want one shareholder with 10% interest to kill the deal. You should seek an agreement that can balance the rights of the

majority and the minority. If a 10% owner is the only one who does not want to sell, then he or she can be given the right to buy out the other 90%.

Devoting Best Efforts

One problem that sometimes comes up in the life of a corporation is that one shareholder loses interest and no longer contributes the time that was originally expected. Another problem may arise when a shareholder becomes a part of a competing enterprise. To avoid disagreements, you should spell out what is expected of each shareholder. You could spell out how many hours a week each person is expected to work, or you could just have a general agreement that each shareholder will devote his or her best efforts to the company.

Right to Serve as Director

A very effective protection for minority shareholders is the right of each to serve as a director. This enables them to take part in directors' meetings without being elected and to stay informed of activities of the corporation. However, being a director does not guarantee a right to control decisions.

Salary

If there is a chance that some of the shareholders will later vote themselves higher salaries than others, you can include an agreement as to what the salaries will be and include a requirement that any change must be agreed to by everyone or by more than a simple majority.

Nominating Officers and Employees

One common provision in a Shareholder Agreement is to agree on what office will be held by each shareholder. Any change could require unanimous consent or a supermajority vote. However, be sure to provide for the possibility that someone may become unable or unwilling to do the job.

Compulsory Buyout

A way to end a dispute between shareholders is to provide for a *compulsory buyout*. This can be *open-ended*, in which either party can buy out the other, or it can be *specific*, in which one person's shares are subject to a buyout. A formula for determining the buyout price should be in the agreement, to avoid disagreements later.

Transfer of Shares

Most small corporations limit the ability of shareholders to sell their shares. This protects the corporation from violations of securities laws and from persons whom they might not want as shareholders. A limitation on the ability to sell shares is usually combined with a buyout plan.

Additional Shares

To maintain a balance of power among the shareholders, it is important to have provisions covering the issuance of new shares or a merger with another corporation. Besides a clause that provides a majority or unanimous consent for decisions concerning these events, a provision to issue new shares on a *pro rata* basis can solve some situations.

Transfer of Substantial Assets

To protect the shareholders' value, a clause should be added that any transfer of substantial assets for any consideration other than cash is not allowed.

Endorsement

An *endorsement* on the shares informs a potential transferee about the circumstance that the shares are subject to certain restrictions concerning their transfer. It warns the transferee and betters the chances of the corporation in case of a lawsuit due to a transfer not being in accordance with the provisions of the Shareholder Agreement.

Formalities

To avoid any misunderstanding, the formalities as to how the Shareholder Agreement should be complied with can be included.

Arbitration

Because going to court is so expensive and can take years, it is a good idea to put an *arbitration* clause in your agreement. Arbitrators, who mediate legal disagreements and issue decisions on them, are often lawyers or former judges, so you get a decision similar to what you would have gotten in court, without the expense or delay.

Boilerplate

Most Shareholder Agreements contain standard legal *boilerplate* language, such as *entire agreement* (there are no verbal additions to this agreement), *severability* (if one clause is invalid that would not be reason to throw out the entire agreement), and *choice of law* (which state's laws will be used to interpret the agreement).

ORGANIZATIONAL PAPERWORK

Every corporation must have *bylaws* and must maintain a set of *minutes* of its meetings. The bylaws must be adopted at the first meeting and the first minutes of the corporation will record the proceedings of the organizational meeting.

Waiver of Notice

Before any meeting of the incorporators, board of directors, or shareholders can be held, formal notice must be given to the parties of the meeting. Since small corporations often need to have meetings on short notice and do not want to be bothered with formal notices, it is customary to have all parties sign written waivers of notice. **WAIVERS OF NOTICE** are included for the organizational meeting and for the annual and special meetings. (see forms 3, 12, 14, 16, and 18.)

Bylaws

The *bylaws* are the rules for organization and operation of the corporation. They are required by state law. Appendix C contains one form of Bylaws for a simple corporation. (see form 5, p.187.) To complete it, fill in the name and state of the corporation, the city of the main office of the corporation, the proposed date of the annual meeting (this can vary each year, as needed), and the number of directors to be on the board.

Minutes

As part of the formal requirements of operating a corporation, *minutes* must be kept of the meetings of shareholders and the board of directors. Usually only one meeting of each is required each year, unless there is some special need for a meeting in the interim (such as the resignation of an officer). The first minutes will be the minutes of the organizational meeting of the corporation. At this meeting, the officers and directors are elected; the bylaws, corporate seal, and stock certificates are adopted; and, other organizational decisions are made. Several **MINUTE** forms are included in Appendix C. (see forms 4, 13, 15, 17, and 19.)

Resolutions

When the board of directors or shareholders make major decisions, it is usually done in the form of a *resolution*. At the organizational meeting, some important resolutions that may be passed are choosing a bank and adopting S corporation status. (see forms 6, 8, and 11 in Appendix C.)

TAX FORMS

Prior to opening a bank account, the corporation must obtain an *Employer Identification Number,* which is the corporate equivalent of a Social Security number. This is done by filing an **APPLICATION FOR EMPLOYER IDENTIFICATION NUMBER (IRS FORM SS-4)**. (see form 2, p.173.)

If you mail this form in, it can take weeks, but you can get your number within a day by phoning the number in the instructions. You will need to have the form completed and in front of you when you call, and you may need to fax the sheet to them. The phone number to obtain the EIN is 800-829-4933.

You may also file online. Go to **www.irs.gov** and search the term "SS-4 online." Follow the instructions for completing the form as you would for a written application. You will receive your EIN shortly thereafter electronically, with a paper receipt mailed to you within two weeks.

When you apply for this number, you will probably be put on the mailing list for other corporate tax forms. If you do not receive these, you should call your local IRS office and request the forms for new businesses. These include *Circular E* (which explains the taxes due), *W-4 forms* for each employee, tax deposit coupons, and *Form 941* quarterly return for withholding.

IRS Form 2553

If your corporation is to be taxed as an S corporation, you must file an **ELECTION BY A SMALL BUSINESS CORPORATION (IRS FORM 2553)** with the IRS within seventy-five days of incorporation. (see form 10, p.203.) As a practical matter, you should sign and file this at your incorporation meeting; otherwise, you may forget.

State Tax Forms

In most states, there is a state corporate income tax. In some states, you will be exempt from corporate income tax if you are an S corporation, but you will need to file a form to let them know that you are exempt.

If you will be selling or renting goods or services at retail, you may be required to collect state sales and use taxes. To do this, you will need to register, and in most cases, pay a registration fee. In some states and in some businesses, you will be required to post a bond covering the taxes you will be collecting. There may be other taxes that your state requires. Contact your state taxing authority and ask for the forms available for new corporations.

CORPORATE SUPPLIES

A corporation needs to keep a permanent record of its legal affairs. This includes: the original Articles of Incorporation; minutes of all meetings; records of the stock issued, transferred, and cancelled; fictitious names registered; and any other legal matters. The records are usually kept in a ring binder. Any ring binder will do, but it is possible to purchase a specially prepared *corporate kit*, which has the name of the corporation printed on it and usually contains some forms, such as minutes and stock certificates. Most of these items are included with this book, so purchasing such a kit is unnecessary unless you want to have a fancy leather binder or specially printed stock certificates.

Some sources for corporate kits include the following.

Blumberg Excelsior
4435 Old Winter Garden Road
Orlando, FL 32811
407-299-8220
800-327-9220
Fax: 407-291-6912
www.blumberg.com/index2.html

Corpex
1440 Fifth Avenue
Bay Shore, NY 11706
800-221-8181
Fax: 800-826-7739
Email: Corpex@CorpexNet.com
www.corpexnet.com

CorpKit Legal Supplies
46 Taft Avenue
Islip, NY 11751
888-888-9120
Fax: 888-777-4617
Email: info@corpkit.com
www.corpkit.com

Corporate Seal   One thing that is not included with this book is a *corporate seal*. This must be specially made for each corporation. Most corporations use a metal seal like a notary's seal to emboss the paper. This can be ordered from an office supply company. Some states now allow rubber stamps for corporate seals. These are cheaper, lighter, and easier to read. Rubber stamp seals can also be ordered from office supply stores, printers, and specialized rubber stamp companies. The corporate seal should contain the full, exact name of the corporation, the word "SEAL," and the year of incorporation. It may be round or rectangular.

Stock Certificates and Offers to Purchase Stock

In some states, corporations are no longer required to issue **Stock Certificates** to represent shares of ownership. (see form 23, p.235.) However, as a practical matter, it is a good idea to do so. This shows some formality and gives each person tangible evidence of ownership. If you do issue shares, the face of each certificate must show the corporate name; the state law under which the corporation is organized; the name of the shareholder(s); and, the number, class, and series of the stock. The certificate must be signed by one or more officers designated by the bylaws or the board of directors.

If there are two or more classes or series of stock, the front or back of the certificate must disclose that, "upon request and without charge, the corporation will provide to the shareholder the preferences, limitations, and relative rights of each class or series, the preferences of any preferred stock, and the board of director's authority to determine rights for any subsequent classes or series." If there are any restrictions, they must be stated on the certificate, or a statement must be included that a copy of the restrictions is available without charge.

The stock certificates can be fancy and intricately engraved with eagles and scrolls, or they can be typed or even handwritten. If you purchase a corporate kit, you will receive certificates printed with your company's name on them. (Ready-to-use stock certificates are included in Appendix C.)

Before any stock is issued, the purchaser should submit an **Offer to Purchase Stock**. (see form 7, p.197.) The **Offer to Purchase Stock** states that the offer is made pursuant to Section 1244 of the Internal Revenue Code. The advantage of this section is that in the event the business fails or the value of the stock drops, the shareholder can write off up to $50,000 ($100,000 for married couples) as ordinary income, rather than as a long-term capital loss, which would be limited to $3,000 a year.

Some thought should be given to the way in which the ownership of the stock will be held. Stock owned in one person's name alone is subject to probate upon death. Making two people joint owners of the stock (joint tenants with full rights of survivorship) would avoid probate upon the death of one of them. However, taking a joint owner's name off in the event of a disagreement (such as divorce) could be troublesome. If a couple jointly operates a business, joint ownership is best. But if one person is the sole party involved in the business, the desire to avoid probate should be weighed against the risk of losing half the business in a divorce.

Most states allow securities to be registered in *pay on death* or *transfer on death* form, similar to bank accounts. This means the stock can be owned by one person, but designated to pass to another person at death without that person getting any current rights in the stock. Check with your stock broker, attorney, or in your state statutes. The law is called the *Uniform TOD Securities Registration Act.* All states have passed this law with the exception of Louisiana, New York, and Texas.

Taxes   Some states levy a tax on the issue or transfer of stock. The amount and means of calculating the tax vary from state to state. Check with the Secretary of State or your county government tax office to find out if any such tax is charged, how to calculate the amount of tax, and how to go about paying it.

This is a tax you can easily lower, but do not avoid paying it. If you do, someone may use this to *pierce the corporate veil* and hold you liable for debts of the corporation. You can keep the tax low by structuring your corporate stock to the minimum tax. In some states, this means fewer shares, and in other states it means lower par value.

Example:
In Ohio, the tax is on the number of shares. To keep the tax low, you would issue a small number of shares and pay a higher

amount for each share. In Florida, the tax is based on the payment for the shares, so you could issue a large number of shares with a low par value. If you wanted to contribute more capital to the corporation, you should designate it as *paid-in surplus* rather than as payment for more shares.

The Ohio tax is $.10 per share for the first thousand shares, with a minimum tax of $85. This means you can have 850 shares without paying extra tax. A person forming an Ohio corporation with $5,000 in capital could authorize 850 shares at $2 par value, issue five hundred, and pay $10 per share.

Florida does not have a tax on authorized shares, but has a documentary stamp tax on issued shares. Thus you could authorize one million shares at $0.001 par value and pay $1000 for all million shares. Additional capital could be contributed as paid-in surplus or as a loan to the corporation.

ORGANIZATIONAL MEETING

The real birth of the corporation takes place at the initial meeting of the incorporators and the initial board of directors. At this meeting, the stock is issued and the officers and board of directors are elected. Other business may also take place, such as opting for S corporation status or adopting employee benefit plans.

Usually, forms for minutes, stock certificates, taxes, and so on are prepared before the organizational meeting and used as a script for the meeting. They are then signed at the end of the meeting.

Several items in the following agenda are forms found in Appendix C. These forms may be torn from the book, photocopied, or rewritten as necessary to fit your situation. They are all also included on the attached CD-ROM for ease of modification.

The agenda for the initial meeting is usually as follows.

1. Sign the **WAIVER OF NOTICE OF ORGANIZATIONAL MEETING** (see form 3, p.181)

2. Note persons present

3. Present and accept the **ARTICLES OF INCORPORATION** (the copy returned by the Secretary of State) (see Appendix B)

4. Elect the directors

5. Adopt the **BYLAWS** (see form 5, p.187)

6. Elect the officers

7. Present and accept the corporate seal

8. Present and accept the **STOCK CERTIFICATES** (see form 23, p.235)

9. Adopt the **BANKING RESOLUTION** (see form 6, p.195)

10. Adopt the resolution accepting stock offers

11. Adopt the **RESOLUTION TO REIMBURSE EXPENSES** (see form 8, p.199)

12. Adopt any special resolutions such as **ELECTION BY A SMALL BUSINESS CORPORATION (IRS FORM 2553)** (see form 10, p.203)

13. Adjourn

The stock certificates are usually issued at the end of the meeting, but in some cases, such as when a prospective shareholder does not yet have money to pay for them, they are issued when paid for.

To issue the stock, the certificates in Appendix C should be completed by adding the name of the corporation, the state of incorporation, the number of shares the certificate represents, and the person to whom the certificate is issued. Each certificate should be numbered in order to keep track of it.

A record of the stock issuance should be made on the **STOCK TRANSFER LEDGER** and on the **STOCK CERTIFICATE STUBS**. (see form 21, p.229 and form 22, p.231.) The **STOCK CERTIFICATE STUBS** should be cut apart on the dotted lines, punched, and inserted in the ring binder. Some states may charge taxes or fees upon the issuance of stock. You should check with your Secretary of State's office to determine all necessary taxes or fees. (see Appendix A.)

MINUTE BOOK

After the organizational meeting, you should set up your minute book. As noted previously, this can be a fancy leather book or a simple ring binder. The minute book usually contains the following.

1. Title page ("Corporate Records of _____")

2. Table of contents

3. The letter from the Secretary of State acknowledging receipt and filing of the Articles of Incorporation

4. Copy of the **ARTICLES OF INCORPORATION** (see Appendix B)

5. Copy of any fictitious name registration

6. Copy of any trademark registration

7. **WAIVER OF NOTICE OF ORGANIZATIONAL MEETING** (see form 3, p.181)

8. **MINUTES OF ORGANIZATIONAL MEETING** (see form 4, p.183)

9. **BYLAWS** (see form 5, p.187)

10. Sample **STOCK CERTIFICATE** (see form 23, p.235)

11. **OFFER TO PURCHASE STOCK** (see form 7, p.197)

12. Tax forms:

    a. **IRS FORM SS-4** (form 2) identifying the issued Employer Identification Number

    b. **IRS FORM 2553** (form 10) and acceptance notification from the IRS

    c. Any state form necessary, along with state tax number

13. **STOCK TRANSFER LEDGER** (see form 21, p.229)

14. **STOCK CERTIFICATE STUBS** (see form 22, p.231)

BANK ACCOUNT

A corporation will need a bank account. Typically, checks payable to a corporation cannot be cashed by a shareholder. Instead, they must be deposited into an account.

Bank Fees Unfortunately, many banks charge ridiculous rates to corporations for the right to put their money in the bank. You can tell how much extra a corporation is being charged when you compare a corporate account with a personal account with similar activity.

Fortunately, some banks have set up reasonable fees for small corporations. Some charge no fees if a balance of $1,000 or $2,500 is maintained. Because the fees can easily amount to hundreds of dollars a year, it pays to shop around. Even if the bank is relatively far from the business, using bank-by-mail and online banking can make the distance meaningless.

Another way to save money in bank charges is to order checks from a private source rather than through the bank. These are usually much cheaper than the checks the bank offers, because most banks get a commission on check orders. If the bank officer does not like the idea when you are opening the account, just wait until your first batch of bank checks runs out and switch over at that time.

Paperwork   All you should need to open a corporate bank account is a copy of your Articles of Incorporation and your federal tax identification number (and perhaps a business license). If you have trouble opening the account, you can use the **BANKING RESOLUTION** included in Appendix C or one the bank requires (their own form), or you can make up a similar form. (see form 6, p.195.)

LICENSES

In some states, counties and municipalities are authorized to levy a license fee or tax on the privilege of doing business. Before opening your business, you need to find out if any such license is required. Businesses that perform work in several cities, such as builders, may need to obtain a license from each city or county in which they perform work or have an office.

Every state also has laws requiring the licensing of certain types of businesses or professions. Some states regulate more types than others. Just because you did not need a license in one state is not a guarantee that you will not need one if you move to a new state.

Be sure to find out if zoning allows your type of business before buying or leasing property. Usually, the licensing departments will check the zoning before issuing your license.

Selling Corporate Stock

While many people are eager to put money into a startup business and the businesses are even more eager to get it, there is a labyrinth of laws controlling exactly how and from whom you can accept funds. Numerous stock frauds over the years have resulted in harsh criminal penalties for those who do not follow the laws.

SECURITIES LAWS

The issuance of securities is subject to both federal and state securities laws. A *security* is stock in the company (common and preferred) and debt (notes, bonds, etc.). The laws covering securities are so broad that any instrument that represents an investment in an enterprise in which the investor is relying on the efforts of others for profit is considered a security. Even a promissory note has been held to be a security. Once an investment is determined to involve a security, strict rules apply. There can be criminal penalties and civil damages can be awarded to purchasers if the rules are not followed.

The rules are designed to protect people who put up money as an investment in a business. In the stock market crash in the 1930s, many people lost their life savings in swindles, and the government wants to be sure that it will not happen again. Unfortunately, the laws can also make it difficult to raise capital for many honest businesses.

The goal of the laws covering sales of securities is that investors be given full disclosure of the risks involved in an investment. To accomplish this, the law usually requires that the securities must either be registered with the federal *Securities and Exchange Commission* (SEC) or a similar state regulatory body, and that lengthy disclosure statements be compiled and distributed.

The law is complicated and strict compliance is required. You most likely would not be able to get through the registration process on your own. You may wish to consider some alternatives when attempting to raise capital without an attorney.

- Borrow the money as a personal loan from friends or relatives. The disadvantage is that you will have to pay them back personally if the business fails. However, you may have to do that anyway if they are close relatives or if you do not follow the securities laws.

- Tailor your stock issuance to fall within the exemptions in the securities laws. There are some exemptions in the securities laws for small businesses that may apply to your transaction. (The anti-fraud provisions always apply, even if the transaction is exempt from registration.) Some exemptions are explained in the following section, but you should make at least one appointment with a securities lawyer to be sure you have covered everything and that there have not been any changes in the law. You can often pay $100 or $200 for an hour or so of a securities attorney's time and just ask questions about your plans. He or she can tell you what not to do and what your options are. Then you can make an informed decision.

FEDERAL EXEMPTIONS FROM SECURITIES LAWS

In most situations involving one person, a husband and wife, or a few partners running a business, where all parties are active in the enterprise, securities laws do not apply to the issuance of stock to themselves. These are the simple corporations that are the subject of this book. As a practical matter, if your father or aunt wants to put up some money for some stock in your business, you probably will not get in trouble. They probably will not seek triple damages and criminal penalties if your business fails.

However, you may wish to obtain money from additional investors to enable your business to grow. This can be done in many circumstances, as long as you follow the rules carefully. In some cases, you do not have to file anything with the SEC, but in others, you must file a notice.

Federal Private Offering Exemption

If you sell your stock to a small group of people without any advertising, you fall into the *private offering exemption*. Some of the requirements for this exemption include the following.

- ✪ All persons to whom offers are made must be financially astute, participants in the business, or have a substantial net worth.

- ✪ No advertising or general solicitation is used to promote the stock.

- ✪ The number of persons to whom the offers are made is limited.

- ✪ The shares are purchased for investment and not for immediate resale.

- ✪ The persons to whom the stock is offered are given all relevant information (including financial information) regarding the issuance and the corporation.

- ✪ A filing claiming the exemption is made upon the United States Securities and Exchange Commission.

Again, there are numerous court cases explaining each aspect of these rules, including such questions as what is a *financially astute* person.

Federal Intrastate Offering Exemption

If you only offer your securities to residents of one state, you may be exempt from federal securities laws. Federal laws usually only apply to interstate commerce. Intrastate offerings are covered by SEC Rule 147, and if it is followed carefully, your sale will be exempt from federal registration.

Federal Small Offerings Exemptions

In recent years, the Securities and Exchange Commission has liberalized the rules in order to make it easier for business to grow. The SEC has adopted Regulation D, which states that there are three types of exemptions, found in SEC Rules 504, 505, and 506.

SEC Rule 504. Offering of securities of up to $1,000,000 in a twelve-month period can be exempt under SEC Rule 504. Offers can be made to any number of persons, no specific information must be provided, and investors do not have to be sophisticated.

SEC Rule 505. Under SEC Rule 505, offering of up to $5,000,000 can be made in a twelve-month period, but no public advertising may be used and only thirty-five nonaccredited investors may purchase stock. Any number of *accredited investors* may purchase stock. Accredited investors are sophisticated individuals with high net worth or high income, large trusts or investment companies, or persons involved in the business.

SEC Rule 506. SEC Rule 506 has no limit on the amount of money that may be raised, but like Rule 505, does not allow advertising and limits nonaccredited investors to thirty-five.

STATE SECURITIES LAWS

One reason there are exemptions from federal securities laws is because there are so many state laws covering securities that additional registration is not needed. Every state has securities laws, which are called *blue sky laws*. If you wish to offer your stock in all fifty states, you must be registered in all fifty states, unless you can fit into one of the exemptions. However, exemptions are very limited.

Private Placement Exemption

The most common state exemption is the *private placement exemption*. This can apply if all of the following are true:

- ✪ there are thirty-five or fewer purchasers of shares;

- ✪ no commissions are paid to anyone to promote the stock;

- ✪ no advertising or general solicitation is used to promote the stock;

- ✪ all material information (including financial information) regarding the stock issuance and the company is given to or accessible to all shareholders; and,

- ✪ a three-day right of recision is given.

These rules may sound simple on the surface, but there are many rules, regulations, and court cases explaining each one in more detail. For example, what does thirty-five purchasers mean? It sounds simple, but it can mean more than thirty-five persons. Spouses, persons whose net worth exceeds a million dollars, and founders of the corporation may not be counted in some circumstances. Each state has its own blue sky requirements and exemptions. If you are going to raise money from investors, check with a qualified securities lawyer.

As you can see, the exemption does not give you much latitude in raising money. Therefore, you will have to register with the SEC. To find out more about the registration process in each state, contact the office in each state in which you intend to sell stock. The addresses are at the end of this chapter.

INTERNET STOCK SALES

With the advent of the Internet, promoters of stock have a new way of reaching large numbers of people financially able to afford investments in securities. However, all securities laws apply to the Internet, and they are being enforced. Recently, state attorneys general have issued *cease and desist orders* to promoters not registered in their states.

Under current law, you must be registered in a state in order to sell stock to its residents. If you are not registered in a state, you must turn down any residents from that state who want to buy your stock.

PAYMENT FOR SHARES

When issuing stock, it is important that full payment be made by the purchasers. If the shares have a par value and the payment is in cash, then the cash must not be less than the par value. In most states, promissory notes cannot be used in payment for shares. The shares must not be issued until the payment has been received by the corporation.

Trading Property for Shares

In many cases, organizers of a corporation have property they want to contribute for use in starting up the business. This is often the case when an on-going business is incorporated. To avoid future problems, the property should be traded at a fair value for the shares. The directors should pass a resolution stating that they agree with the value of the property. When the stock certificate is issued in exchange for the property, a **BILL OF SALE** should be executed by the owner of the property, detailing everything that is being exchanged for the stock. (see form 9, p.201.)

Taxable Transactions

In cases where property is exchanged for something of value, such as stock, there is often income tax due, as if there had been a sale of the property. Fortunately, the Federal Tax Code allows tax-free exchange of property for stock if the persons receiving the stock for the property or for cash end up owning at least 80% of the voting and other stock in the corporation (Internal Revenue Service Code, Section 351). If more than 20% of the stock is issued in exchange for services instead of property and cash, then the transfers of property will be taxable and treated as a sale for cash.

Trading Services for Shares

In some cases, the founders of a corporation may wish to issue stock to one or more persons in exchange for their services to the corporation. It has always been possible to issue shares for services that have previously been performed. Some states make it unlawful to issue shares for promises to perform services in the future. Check your state's statutes regarding this.

STATE SECURITIES REGISTRATION OFFICES

The following are the addresses of the offices that can supply you with information on securities registration requirements for each state. Toll-free numbers provided are applicable only when dialed within the respective state.

Alabama
Securities Commission
770 Washington Avenue
Suite 570
Montgomery, AL 36130-4700
Phone: 334-242-2984
        800-222-1253
Fax: 334-242-0240
http://asc.state.al.us

Alaska
Department of Community and
    Economic Development
The Division of Banking,
    Securities and Corporations
P.O. Box 110807
Juneau, AK 99811-0807
Phone: 907-465-2521
        888-925-2521
Fax: 907-465-2549
www.dced.state.ak.us/bsc

Arizona
Corporation Commission
Securities Division
1300 West Washington Street
Third Floor
Phoenix, AZ 85007
Phone: 602-542-4242
Fax: 602-594-7470
www.ccsd.cc.state.az.us

Arkansas
Securities Department
Heritage West Building
201 East Markham
Suite 300
Little Rock, AR 72201
Phone: 501-324-9260
Fax: 501-324-9268
www.state.ar.us/arsec

California
Department of Corporations
Securities Regulation Division
320 West 4th Street
Suite 750
Los Angeles, CA 90013
Phone: 866-275-2677
        213-576-7500
Fax: 213-576-7179
www.corp.ca.gov/srd/security.htm

Colorado
Division of Securities
1580 Lincoln Street
Suite 420
Denver, CO 80203
Phone: 303-894-2320
Fax: 303-861-2126
www.dora.state.co.us/Securities

Connecticut
Department of Banking
Securities and Business
 Investments Division
260 Constitution Plaza
Hartford, CT 06103-1800
Phone: 860-240-8230
 800-831-7225
Fax: 860-240-8295
www.state.ct.us/dob

Delaware
Division of Securities
Department of Justice
820 North French Street
5ᵗʰ Floor
Carvel State Office Building
Wilmington, DE 19801
Phone: 302-577-8424
Fax:.302-577-6987
www.state.de.us/securities

District of Columbia
The Department of Insurance
 and Securities Regulation
810 First Street, NE
Suite 701
Washington, DC 20002
Phone: 202-727-8000
Fax: 202-535-1196
http://disb.dc.gov

Florida
Office of Comptroller
Department of Banking
200 East Gaines Street
Tallahassee, FL 32399
Phone: 850-410-9805
Fax: 850-410-9279
www.flofr.com/licensing

Georgia
Office of the Secretary of State
Division of Securities and
 Business Regulation
Two Martin Luther King, Jr.
 Drive, SE
802 West Tower
Atlanta, GA 30334
Phone: 404-656-3920
Fax: 404-657-8410
www.sos.state.ga.us/securities

Hawaii
Department of Commerce and
 Consumer Affairs
P.O. Box 40
Honolulu, HI 96810
Phone: 808-586-2744
Fax: 808-586-3977
www.state.hi.us/dcca

Idaho
Department of Finance
Securities Bureau
700 West State Street
2ⁿᵈ Floor
Boise, ID 83720

Mailing Address:
P.O. Box 83720
Boise, ID 83720-0031
Phone: 208-332-8004
Fax: 208-332-8099
www.state.id.us/finance/sec.htm

Illinois
Office of the Secretary of State
Securities Department
69 West Washington Street
Suite 1220
Chicago, IL 60602
Phone: 312-793-3384
      800-628-7937
Fax: 312-793-1202

Springfield Office:
Jefferson Terrace
Suite 300 A
300 West Jefferson Street
Springfield, IL 62702
Phone: 217-782-2256
Fax: 217-782-8876
www.sos.state.il.us

Indiana
Office of the Secretary of State
Securities Division
302 West Washington Street
Room E-111
Indianapolis, IN 46204
Phone: 317-232-6681
      800-223-8791
Fax: 317-233-3675
www.in.gov/sos/securities/
  index.html

Iowa
Insurance Division
Securities Bureau
330 Maple Street
Des Moines, IA 50319-0065
Phone: 515-281-5705
Fax: 515-281-3059
www.iid.state.ia.us

Kansas
Office of the Securities
  Commissioner
618 South Kansas Avenue
Topeka, KS 66603-3804
Phone: 785-296-3307
      800-232-9580
Fax: 785-296-6872
www.securities.state.ks.us

Kentucky
Kentucky Office of Financial
  Institutions
Division of Securities
1025 Capital Center Drive
Suite 200
Frankfort, KY 40601
Phone: 502-573-3390
      800-223-2579
Fax: 502-573-8787
www.dfi.state.ky.us

Louisiana
Securities Commission
P.O. Box 94095
Baton Rouge, LA 70804
Phone: 225-925-4660
Fax: 225-925-4548
www.ofi.state.la.us

Maine
Department of Professional and
  Financial Regulation
Office of Securities
121 State House Station
Augusta, ME 04333
Phone: 207-624-8551
Fax: 207-624-8590
www.state.me.us/pfr/sec/
  sec_index.htm

Maryland
Office of the Attorney General
Division of Securities
200 St. Paul Place
Baltimore, MD 21202
Phone: 410-576-6360
Fax: 410-576-6532
www.oag.state.md.us/Securities/
    index.htm

Massachusetts
Secretary of the Commonwealth
Securities Division
One Ashburton Place
17th Floor
Boston, MA 02108
Phone: 617-727-3548
        800-269-5428
Fax: 617-248-0177
www.sec.state.ma.us/sct/
    sctidx.htm

Michigan
Office of Financial and
    Insurance Services
Division of Securities
P.O. Box 30220
Lansing, MI 48909
Phone: 877-999-6442
        517-373-0220
Fax: 517-241-6356
www.michigan.gov/ofis

Minnesota
Department of Commerce
Securities Division
85 Seventh Place East
Suite 500
St. Paul, MN 55101
Phone: 651-296-4973
        651-296-4026
Fax: 651-297-1959
        Attn: Securities
www.state.mn.us/cgi-bin/
    portal/mn/jsp/home.do?
    agency=Commerce

Mississippi
Secretary of State's Office
Business Regulation and
    Enforcement Division
700 North Street
Jackson, MS 39202

Mailing Address:
P.O. Box 136
Jackson, MS 39205
Phone: 800-804-6364
Fax: 601-359-2663
www.sos.state.ms.us/regenf/
    securities/securities.asp

Missouri
Office of the Secretary of State
Securities Division
600 West Main Street
Jefferson City, MO 65101
Phone: 573-751-4136
Fax: 573-526-3124
http://sos.state.mo.us/securities

Montana
Office of the State Auditor
Securities Department
840 Helena Avenue
Helena, MT 59601
Phone: 406-444-2040
        800-332-6148
Fax: 406-444-5558
www.state.mt.us/sao/securities/
    secintro.htm

Nebraska
Department of Banking and
    Finance
Bureau of Securities
1230 O Street
Suite 400
Lincoln, NE 68508

Mailing Address:
P.O. Box 95006
Lincoln, NE 68509-5006
Phone: 402-471-3445
www.ndbf.org

Nevada
Secretary of State
Securities Division
555 East Washington Street
Suite 5200
Las Vegas, NV 89101
Phone: 702-486-2440
Fax: 702-486-2452

Reno Office:
Securities Satellite Office
1755 East Plumb Lane
Suite 231
Reno, NV 89502
Phone: 775-688-1855
Fax: 775-688-1858
http://sos.state.nv.us/securities

New Hampshire
Bureau of Securities Regulation
State House Annex
Room 317A
Concord, NH 03301

Mailing Address:
Bureau of Securities Regulation
Department of State
State House
Room 204
Concord, NH 03301-4989
Phone: 603-271-1463
Fax: 603-271-7933
http://webster.state.nh.us/sos/
    securities

New Jersey
Division of Consumer Affairs
Bureau of Securities
153 Halsey Street
6th Floor
Newark, NJ 07102

Mailing Address:
P.O. Box 47029
Newark, NJ 07101
Phone: 973-504-3600
        866-838-6240
Fax: 973-504-3601
www.state.nj.us/lps/ca/bos.htm

New Mexico
Securities Division
2550 Cerrillos Road
Santa Fe, NM 87505
Phone: 505-476-4580
      800-704-5533
Fax: 505-984-0617
www.rld.state.nm.us/Securities/
  index.htm

New York
Office of the Attorney General
Investor Protection Securities
  Bureau
120 Broadway
23rd Floor
New York, NY 10271
Phone: 212-416-8000
Fax: 212-416-8816
www.oag.state.ny.us

North Carolina
P.O. Box 29622
Raleigh, NC 27626-0622
Phone: 919-733-3924
      800-688-4507
Fax: 919-821-0818
www.secretary.state.nc.us/sec

North Dakota
Securities Commissioner
State Capitol Building
5th Floor
600 East Boulevard Avenue
Bismarck, ND 58505-0510
Phone: 701-328-2910
      800-297-5124
Fax: 701-328-2946
www.state.nd.us/securities
www.ndsecurities.com

Ohio
Division of Securities
77 South High Street
22nd Floor
Columbus, OH 43215
Phone: 614-644-7381
      800-788-1194
Fax: 614-466-3316
www.securities.state.oh.us

Oklahoma
Department of Securities
Suite 860, First National Center
120 North Robinson
Oklahoma City, OK 73102
Phone: 405-280-7700
Fax: 405-280-7742
www.securities.state.ok.us

Oregon
Department of Consumer and
  Business Services
Division of Finance and
  Corporate Securities
350 Winter Street, NE
Room 410
Salem, OR 97301-3881
Phone: 503-378-4140
Fax: 503-947-7862
www.oregondfcs.org

Pennsylvania
Securities Commission
http://sites.state.pa.us/PA_Exec/
  Securities

Harrisburg Office:
Eastgate Office Building
2nd Floor
1010 North Seventh Street
Harrisburg, PA 17102-1410
Phone: 717-787-8061
Fax: 717-783-5122

Philadelphia Office:
1109 State Office Building
Philadelphia, PA 19130-4088
Phone: 215-560-2088
Fax: 215-560-3977

Pittsburgh Office:
806 State Office Building
Pittsburgh, PA 15222-1210
Phone: 412-565-5083
Fax: 412-565-7646

Puerto Rico
Commissioner of Financial
   Institutions
P.O. Box 11855
San Juan, Puerto Rico 00910
Phone: 787-723-3131
Fax: 787-723-4225
www.ocif.gobierno.pr/valores_
   eng.html

Rhode Island
Department of Business
   Regulation
Securities Division
233 Richmond Street
Suite 232
Providence, RI 02903
Phone: 401-222-3048
Fax: 401-222-5629
www.dbr.state.ri.us

South Carolina
Office of the S.C. Attorney
   General
Securities Division
Rembert C. Dennis Office
   Building
1000 Assembly Street
Columbia, SC 29201

Mailing Address:
P.O. Box 11549
Columbia, SC 29211-1549
Phone: 803-734-9916
Fax: 803-734-3677
www.scsecurities.com

South Dakota
Division of Securities
445 East Capitol Avenue
Pierre, SD 57501
Phone: 605-773-4823
Fax: 605-773-5953
www.state.sd.us/dcr/securities

Tennessee
Department of Commerce and
   Insurance
Securities Division
500 James Robertson Parkway
Suite 680
Nashville, TN 37243
Phone: 615-741-2947
        800-863-9117
Fax: 615-532-8375
www.state.tn.us/commerce/
   securities/index.html

Texas
State Securities Board
Rusk Building
208 East 10th Street
5th Floor
Austin, TX 78701

Mailing Address:
P.O. Box 13167
Austin, TX 78711-3167
Phone: 512-305-8300
Fax: 512-305-8310
www.ssb.state.tx.us

Utah
Division of Securities
160 East 300 South
2nd Floor
Salt Lake City, UT 84111

Mailing Address:
Box 146760
Salt Lake City, UT 84114-6760
Phone: 801-530-6600
Fax: 801-530-6980
www.securities.state.ut.us

Vermont
Department of Banking,
   Insurance, Securities
   and Health Care
Securities Division
89 Main Street
Drawer 20
Montpelier, VT 05620-3101
Phone: 802-828-3420
Fax: 802-828-2896
www.bishca.state.vt.us/
   SecuritiesDiv/securindex.htm

Virginia
State Corporation Division
Division of Securities and Retail
   Franchising
Tyler Building
9th Floor
1300 East Main Street
Richmond, VA 23219

Mailing Address:
P.O. Box 1197
Richmond, VA 23218
Phone: 804-371-9051
          800-552-7945
Fax: 804-371-9911
www.state.va.us/scc/division/srf

Washington
Department of Financial
   Institutions
Securities Division
150 Israel Road SW
Tumwater, WA 98501

Mailing Address:
P.O. Box 41200
Olympia, WA 98504
Phone: 360-902-8700
          800-372-8303
Fax: 360-902-0524
www.wa.gov/dfi/securities

West Virginia
Office of the State Auditor
Securities Commission
State Capitol Building 1
Room W-100
Charleston, WV 25305
Phone: 304-558-2257
        888-368-9507
Fax: 304-558-4211
www.wvauditor.com/securities/
   securities.shtml

Wisconsin
Department of Financial
   Institutions
Division of Securities
345 West Washington Avenue
Madison, WI 53703

Mailing Address:
P.O. Box 1768
Madison, WI 53701-1768
Phone: 608-266-1064
Fax: 608-264-7979
www.wdfi.org/fi/securities

Wyoming
Secretary of State
Securities Division
State Capitol Building
Room 109
200 West 24th Street
Cheyenne, WY 82002
Phone: 307-777-7370
Fax: 307-777-5339
http://soswy.state.wy.us/securiti/
   securiti.htm

Running a Corporation

One of the rules for running a corporation is that you should follow the formalities of the corporation if you wish to be treated as a corporation. You should follow these formalities on a daily basis and not just create the paperwork if you are sued.

DAY-TO-DAY ACTIVITIES

There are not many differences between running a corporation and any other type of business. The most important point to remember is to keep the corporation's affairs separate from your personal affairs. The corporation should not make frequent loans to its shareholders, and funds of the corporation and individual shareholders should not be commingled. Funds taken out or put into the corporation should be documented. The decision of whether these should be salary, loans, dividends, or otherwise, should be made with the help of an accountant or good tax guide based upon your financial situation.

Another important point to remember is to always refer to the corporation as a corporation. *Always* use the complete corporate name, including designations such as Inc. or Corp., on *everything*. *Always* sign corporate documents with your corporate title. If you do not, you may lose your protection from liability. There have been many cases in which a person forgot to put the word pres. or president after his or her name when entering into contracts for the corporation. As a result, the person was determined to be personally liable for performance of the contract.

CORPORATE RECORDS

A corporation must keep minutes of the proceedings of its shareholders, board of directors, and committees of directors. The minutes should be in writing. Some states allow minutes to be kept in forms other than writing, provided they can be converted into written form within a reasonable time. This would mean that they could be kept in a computer or possibly on a videotape. However, it is always best to keep a duplicate copy or at least one written copy. Accidents can easily erase magnetic media.

Record of Shareholders

The corporation must also keep a record of its shareholders, including their names and addresses, and the number, class, and series of shares owned. This can be kept at the registered office, principal place of business, or office of its stock transfer agent (if any). A **STOCK TRANSFER LEDGER** can be found in Appendix C. (see form 21, p.229.)

Examination of Records

Any shareholder of a corporation has the right to examine and copy the corporation's books and records, after giving proper notice before the date on which he or she wishes to inspect and copy. The shareholder must have a good faith reason to inspect. He or she must describe his or her purpose, the records he or she wishes to inspect, and how the purpose is related to the records.

The shareholder may have his or her attorney or agent examine the records, and may receive photocopies of the records. The corporation may charge a reasonable fee for making photocopies. If the records are not in written form, the corporation must convert them to written form. Customarily, the corporation must bear the cost of converting all of the following to written form:

- ✪ the Articles of Incorporation and any amendments;

- ✪ the bylaws and any amendments;

- ✪ resolutions by the board of directors creating different rights in the stock;

- ✪ minutes of all shareholders' meetings;

- ✪ records of any action taken by the shareholders without a meeting for the past three years;

- ✪ written communications to all shareholders;

- ✪ names and addresses of all officers and directors; and,

- ✪ the most recent report filed with the state corporate office.

The shareholder may be required to pay for converting any other records to writing.

If the corporation refuses to allow a shareholder to examine the records, most states allow the shareholder to seek an order from the appropriate state court. In such a case, the corporation would normally have to pay the shareholder's costs and attorney's fees.

Balance Sheets   Most states require a corporation to furnish its shareholders with financial statements. This includes an end-of-the-year balance sheet and yearly income and cash flow statements, unless exempted by shareholder resolution.

ANNUAL MEETINGS

Each year, the corporation must hold annual meetings of the shareholders and directors. These meetings may be formal and held in the office, or they may be informal and held in a restaurant. A sole officer and director can hold them in his or her mind without verbally reciting all of the motions or taking a formal vote. The important thing is that the meetings are held and that minutes are kept, even by a one-person corporation.

Regular minutes and meetings are evidence that the corporation is legitimate if the issue ever comes up in court. Minute forms for the annual meetings are included with this book. You can use them as master copies to photocopy each year. The CD-ROM attached to the back cover also contains these forms. When completing them each year, all that needs to be changed is the date, unless you actually change officers or directors, or need to take some other corporate action.

ANNUAL REPORT

Most states require that every corporation file an *annual report* each year. Many states make this a biannual requirement. Fortunately, this is a simple, often one-page form that is sent to the corporation by the Secretary of State, and may merely need to be signed. It contains such information as the federal tax identification number, officers' and directors' names and addresses, the registered agent's name, and the address of the registered office. It must be signed and returned with the required fee by the date specified by the state. If this is not done, then the corporation is dissolved after notice is given. Many states allow some corporate information (such as the registered office and agent) to be changed at this time without additional fees to the corporation. The corporation should be aware of this fact in order to avoid incurring needless expenses.

Amending Corporate Information

Occasionally, a corporation will find that its documents do not meet its current needs. To solve this, they can be amended, but the amendments must be done in compliance with the laws of your state of incorporation.

ARTICLES OF AMENDMENT

The **ARTICLES OF INCORPORATION** included in Appendix B of this book are very basic. Therefore, they would not have to be amended except to change something major, such as the name of the corporation or the number of shares of stock. If the amendment is made before any shares are issued, it may be done by the incorporator or directors by filing an amendment to the Articles, referred to as *Articles of Amendment, Certificate of Amendment,* or some similar title. This will be referred to as *Articles of Amendment* in this book.

These are usually signed by the incorporators or director. They state the name of the corporation, the amendment, the date adopted, and a statement that it is made before the issue of any shares. If the amendment is made after shares have been issued, then the Articles of

Amendment must be signed by the appropriate officers. If the change affects the outstanding shares, then a statement must be included describing how the change will be effected.

The Articles of Amendment must be filed with the corporate filing division along with the appropriate filing fee. The fee for increasing the number of shares that the corporation is authorized to issue is more costly in many states than other amendments. The procedure for filing the Articles of Amendment depends upon who is doing the amending and at what point in time the amendment is adopted. For more information, refer to your Secretary of State's office or your state's corporation laws.

BYLAWS

The shareholders may always amend the bylaws. The board of directors may amend the bylaws unless the Articles of Incorporation state otherwise, or unless the shareholders provide that the bylaws may not be amended by the board.

The Articles of Incorporation may allow a bylaw that requires a greater quorum or voting requirement for shareholders, but such a requirement may not be adopted, amended, or repealed by the board of directors. A bylaw that fixes a greater quorum or voting requirement for the board of directors, and that was adopted by the shareholders, may be amended or repealed only by the shareholders. If it was adopted by the board, it may be amended or repealed only by the board.

REGISTERED AGENT OR REGISTERED OFFICE

To change the registered agent or registered office, a form must be sent to the Secretary of State along with the appropriate fee. Most states provide a form for such a change. The **CHANGE OF REGISTERED AGENT AND/OR REGISTERED OFFICE** form can be used to change both the registered agent and the registered office, or to just change one of them. (see form 20, p.227.) If you are just changing one, such as the agent, then list the registered office as both the old address and the new address.

OFFICERS AND DIRECTORS

Usually, officers and directors are replaced by having an election for new ones. However, if an officer or director wishes to resign before the end of a term, you can use the **OFFICER/DIRECTOR RESIGNATION**. (see form 25, p.253.)

Checklist for Forming a Simple Corporation

❏ Decide on corporate name.

❏ Prepare and file **ARTICLES OF INCORPORATION**. (see Appendix B.)

❏ Complete and file **APPLICATION FOR EMPLOYER IDENTIFICATION NUMBER (IRS FORM SS-4)**. (see form 2, p.173.)

❏ Prepare **SHAREHOLDER AGREEMENT**, if necessary. (see form 24, p.249.)

❏ Meet with accountant to discuss capitalization and tax planning.

❏ If necessary, meet with securities lawyer regarding stock sales.

❏ Obtain corporate seal and ring binder for minutes.

❏ Pay any applicable taxes for sale or issuance of stock.

❏ Hold organizational meeting.

    ❏ Complete **BYLAWS, WAIVERS, MINUTES, OFFERS TO PURCHASE STOCK**. (see forms 3–5, 7, 12–19.)

    ❏ Sign all documents and place in minute book.

❏ Issue stock certificates.

    ❏ Be sure consideration is paid.

    ❏ Complete **BILL OF SALE** if property is traded for stock. (see form 9, p.201.)

❏ File fictitious name if one will be used.

❏ Get licenses.

❏ Open bank account.

❏ For S corporation status, file **IRS FORM 2553**. (see form 10, p.203.)

Glossary

A

annual report. A document filed by a corporation each year, usually listing the officers, directors, and registered agent.

articles of incorporation. The document that demonstrates the organization of a corporation, called certificate of incorporation or charter in some states.

articles of organization. The document that demonstrates the organization of a limited liability company.

B

blue sky laws. Laws governing the sales of securities.

board of directors. Governing body of a corporation that establishes corporate policies, appoints executive officers, and makes major financial decisions.

bylaws. Rules governing the conduct of affairs of a corporation.

C

C corporation. A corporation that pays taxes on its profits.

common stock. The basic ownership shares of a corporation.

contract. An agreement between two or more parties.

corporation. An organization recognized as a legal person that is set up to conduct a business owned by shareholders and run by officers and directors.

D

distributions. Money paid out to owners of a corporation or limited liability company.

domestic corporation. Incorporated in the state in which business is done.

E

employee. Person who works for another under that person's control and direction.

employer identification number. Number issued by the Internal Revenue Service to identify business taxpayers.

estate planning. Preparing documents such as a will, trust, and other arrangements to control the passing of one's property at death.

exemption. The ability to sell certain limited types of securities without full compliance with securities registration laws.

F

fictitious name. A name used by a business that is not its personal or legal name.

foreign corporation. Incorporated in a state other than where business is done.

G

general partnership. A business that is owned by two or more persons.

I

intangible property. Personal property that does not have physical presence, such as the ownership interest in a corporation.

intellectual property. Legal rights to the products of the mind, such as writings, musical compositions, formulas, and designs.

L

liability. The legal responsibility to pay for an injury.

limited liability company (LLC). An entity recognized as a legal person that is set up to conduct a business owned and run by members.

limited liability partnership. An entity recognized as a legal person that is set up to conduct a business owned and run by professionals, such as attorneys or doctors.

limited partnership. A business that is owned by two or more persons, of which one or more is liable for the debts of the business and one or more has no liability for the debts.

M

minutes. Records of the proceedings of corporate meetings.

N

nonprofit corporation. An entity recognized as a legal person that is set up to run an operation in which none of the profits are distributed to controlling members.

O

occupational license. A government-issued permit to transact business.

officers. Those persons who run the day-to-day affairs of the business; usually include a president, secretary, treasurer, and vice president.

operating agreement. A contract among members of a limited liability company that spells out how the company is to be run.

option. The right to buy stock at a future date, usually at a predetermined price.

organizational meeting. The meeting of the founders of a corporation, in which the company is structured and ready to begin business.

P

par value. A value given to newly-issued stock, which used to have legal significance, but now usually does not relate to anything except, in some states, taxation.

partnership. A business formed by two or more persons.

perpetual existence. Continuance of the business after a partner or owner dies.

personal property. Any type of property other than land and the structures attached to it.

piercing the corporate veil. When a court ignores the structure of a corporation and holds its owners responsible for its debts or liabilities.

professional association (P.A.). An entity recognized as a legal person that is set up to conduct a business of professionals, such as attorneys or doctors.

professional service corporation (P.C.). *See professional association.*

promoters. Persons who start a business venture and usually offer interests for sale to investors.

proprietorship. A business that is owned by one person.

R

registered agent. The person authorized to accept legal papers for a corporation, sometimes called a resident agent.

resident agent. *See registered agent.*

S

S corporation. A corporation in which the profits are taxed to the shareholders.

securities. Interests in a business, such as stocks or bonds.

Securities and Exchange Commission (SEC). Government agency that regulates the buying and selling of stock.

shareholder. Person who owns stock in a corporation.

shareholder agreement. A contract among the owners of a corporation that spells out their rights.

shares. Units of stock in a corporation.

sole proprietorship. Type of business in which one person owns and has sole liability for the company.

stock. Ownership interests in a corporation.

stock certificate. Piece of paper used to represent shares of ownership; designates the number, class, and series of the stock issued.

T

tangible property. Physical personal property, such as desks and tables.

trademark. A name or symbol used to identify the source of goods or services.

transferability. The ability to sell shares of stock in a corporation.

U

usury. Charging an interest rate higher than that allowed by law.

W

withholding. Money taken out of an employee's salary and remitted to the government.

Z

zoning. Governmental regulation controlling the use of a piece of real property.

State-by-State Incorporation Laws

The following pages contain a listing of each state's corporation laws and fees. Because the laws are constantly being changed by state legislatures, you should call before filing your papers to confirm the fees and other requirements. The phone numbers are provided for each state.

In the continued growth of the World Wide Web, more and more state corporation divisions are making their fees and procedures available online. Some states have downloadable forms available, and some even allow you to search their entire database from the comfort of your home or office.

For your convenience, a sample **ARTICLES OF INCORPORATION** form from each state that provides one has been included on the attached CD-ROM. You should still check with your state's department that handles corporate matters to make sure there have not been any changes.

The best websites at the time of publication of this book are included for each state. However, the sites change constantly, so you may need to look a little deeper if your state's site has changed its address.

ALABAMA

Title 10-2B, Alabama Statutes
  Secretary of State
  Corporation Section
  P.O. Box 5616
  Montgomery, AL 36103-5616
  334-242-5324
  Website: www.sos.state.al.us

I. ARTICLES OF INCORPORATION

A. Must file the original and two exact copies of the Articles in the office of the probate judge in the county where the initial registered office of the corporation will be located.

II. THE CORPORATE NAME

A. Name must contain the word corporation, incorporated, or abbreviation of the same.

B. Prior to incorporation, a corporate name may be reserved for a period of 120 days. Name may be reserved by telephone (334-242-5324) or fax (334-240-3138) subject to further Secretary of State requirements.

C. There is no fee charged when initially registering the corporate name. The fee is included with the filing fee. If the name is reserved prior to filing the Articles, no charge is initially assessed. However, if the Articles are not filed within 120 days, the incorporator is billed the $10.00.

III. DIRECTORS

A. Directors must be at least 19 years old, but need not be residents of the state or shareholders of the corporation.

B. The Articles or bylaws may prescribe additional requirements or qualifications.

C. A corporation must have one director or more as initially stated in Articles and thereafter as many directors as stated in bylaws.

D. Director(s) are normally elected at the annual meeting of shareholders.

IV. OFFICERS

A. A corporation has the officers described in its bylaws and appointed or elected in accordance with provisions set forth in the bylaws.

B. The same person may hold more than one office unless provided for otherwise in the bylaws.

C. An officer performs duties stated in the bylaws or by the board of directors or another officer to the extent consistent with the bylaws.

V. REGISTERED AGENT

A. A corporation must register an agent for service of process with the state who has an office within the state.

VI. FILING FEES

A. Articles of Incorporation
    1. State of Alabama $40.00
    2. County Probate Judge $35.00 (each county attaches miscellaneous fees)

B. Application for Name Reservation $10.00 (if Articles not filed as described in II.C. above)

C. Amending Articles of Incorporation
    1. County Probate Judge $10.00
    2. State of Alabama $20.00 (for name change only)

D. Filing Annual Report State of Alabama $10.00
    (minimum fee based on $5000 of capital stock)

E. Cost for Certified Copy of Any Document $1.00/page plus $5.00 to certify the document

NOTE: *The minimum filing fee to initially incorporate is $85.00 for the filing of the Articles and the application for name reservation. Many banks request a certified copy of the Articles prior to setting up a corporate account. Therefore, the certification cost is often necessary as well.*

Expedite service fee $100.00.

ALASKA

Title 10, Alaska Statutes

Department of Community and Economic Development

Division of B.S.C.

Attention: Corporation Section

P.O. Box 110808

Juneau, AK 99811-0808

907-465-2530

907-465-3257 (fax)

Website: www.dced.state.ak.us/bsc/corps.htm

I. ARTICLES OF INCORPORATION

    A. Must be printed or typewritten in English.

    B. Must provide state corporation office with the original and one exact copy of the Articles.

    C. May be filed online at the above website.

II. THE CORPORATE NAME

    A. Name must contain the word corporation, incorporated, company, limited, or abbreviation of the same.

    B. Name must not contain the word city, borough, or village.

    C. Prior to incorporation, a corporate name may be reserved for a period of 120 days.

III. DIRECTORS

    A. Directors need not be residents of the state or shareholders of the corporation.

    B. The Articles or bylaws may prescribe additional requirements or qualifications.

    C. A corporation must have at least one director. If the number of directors is not set, the number of directors shall be three.

    D. Director(s) are normally elected at the annual meeting of shareholders.

IV. OFFICERS

    A. A corporation must have a president, secretary, and treasurer. Other officers may be elected or appointed in accordance with provisions set forth in the bylaws.

    B. The same person may more than one office, except for the office of president and secretary. If all issued stock is owned by one person, he or she may hold all offices.

    C. An officer performs duties stated in the bylaws or by the board of directors or another officer to the extent consistent with the bylaws.

V. REGISTERED AGENT

    A. A corporation must register an agent with the state who has an office within the state.

VI. FILING FEES

A.	Articles of Incorporation	$250.00
B.	Change of Registered Agent and Acceptance	$25.00
C.	Application for Name Reservation	$25.00
D.	Amending Articles of Incorporation	$25.00
E.	Filing Biennial Report	$100.00
F.	Cost for Certified Copy of Articles	$15.00

NOTE: *The filing fees include $150.00 for the actual filing of the Articles and $100.00 for the initial biennial report.*

ARIZONA

Title 10, Arizona Statutes

Arizona Corporation Commission

1300 West Washington

Phoenix, AZ 85007-3026

602-542-3026

800-345-5819 (Arizona residents only)

or

400 West Congress

Tucson, AZ 85701-1347

520-628-6560

Website: www.cc.state.az.us/corp/index.ssi

I. ARTICLES OF INCORPORATION

  A. One person must act as incorporator.

  B. Must provide state corporation office with the original and one exact copy of the Articles. The copy will be returned to the incorporator within 60 days. It must be published for three consecutive publications in a newspaper of general circulation in the county of the known place of business.

  C. May be filed online at the above website.

II. THE CORPORATE NAME

  A. Name must contain the word association, bank, company, corporation, incorporated, limited, or abbreviation of the same. The name must be distinguishable from other corporate names.

  B. Prior to incorporation, a corporate name may be reserved for a period of 120 days.

III. DIRECTORS

  A. Directors need not be residents of the state or shareholders of the corporation.

  B. The Articles or bylaws may prescribe additional requirements or qualifications.

  C. A corporation must have one director or more as initially stated in Articles and thereafter as many directors as stated in bylaws.

  D. Director(s) are normally elected at the annual meeting of shareholders.

IV. OFFICERS

  A. A corporation has the officers described in its bylaws or appointed by the board of directors.

  B. The same person may hold more than one office.

  C. One officer shall be responsible for preparing the records of any director or shareholder meeting.

V. REGISTERED AGENT

  A. Corporation must have a statutory agent at a known place of business within the state.

VI. FILING FEES

A.	Articles of Incorporation	$60.00
B.	Amending Articles of Incorporation	$25.00
C.	Filing Annual Report	$45.00
D.	Cost for Certified Copy of Document	$5.00 + .50/page
E.	Fee for Publishing Articles and Amendments in County of Business	varies based on the newspaper used for publication
F.	Name Reservation	$10.00
G.	Expedited filing within 3–5 business days	$35.00

ARKANSAS

Title 4, Chapter 27, Arkansas Statutes
  Secretary of State
  Corporation Division
  State Capitol
  Room 256
  Little Rock, AR 72201
  501-682-8032
  Website: www.sosweb.state.ar.us

I.   ARTICLES OF INCORPORATION
  A. Must be printed or typewritten in English.
  B. Must provide state corporation office with duplicate originals of the Articles and a completed corporate franchise tax form.
  C. May be filed online at the above website.

II. THE CORPORATE NAME
  A. Name must indicate its corporate character. This can be done by using such words as corporation, incorporated, company, limited, or abbreviation of the same.
  B. Prior to incorporation, a corporate name may be reserved for a period of 120 days.
  C. Foreign corporation may register its corporate name.

III. DIRECTORS
  A. Directors need not be residents of the state or shareholders of the corporation unless bylaws require it.
  B. The Articles or bylaws may prescribe additional requirements or qualifications.
  C. A corporation must have at least one director. The number of directors must be fixed in the manner set forth in the Articles or bylaws.
  D. Director(s) are normally elected at the annual meeting of shareholders unless the terms are staggered.

IV. OFFICERS
  A. A corporation has the officers described in its bylaws or appointed by the board of directors.
  B. An officer performs duties stated in the bylaws or by the board of directors or another officer to the extent consistent with the bylaws.
  C. One officer shall be responsible for preparing the records of any director or shareholder meeting.

V.   REGISTERED AGENT
  A. A corporation must register an agent with the state who is a resident with a physical address in Arkansas; or a corporation with a business office identical with the registered office; or a foreign corporation authorized to do business in Arkansas whose business office is identical with the registered office.

VI. FILING FEES

A.	Articles of Incorporation	$50.00
B.	Change of Registered Agent' Name/Address	$25.00
C.	Application for Name Reservation	$25.00
D.	Amending Articles of Incorporation	$50.00
E.	Filing Annual Report (Minimum)	$50.00
F.	Cost for Certified Copy of Any Document	$5.00 + .50/page

NOTE: *In filing the annual franchise tax report, fee is based on value of stock. Fees are reduced slightly if the filing is done electronically.*

CALIFORNIA

California Corporation Code, Title 1

Secretary of State

Corporate Division

1500 11ᵗʰ Street

Sacramento, CA 95814

916-657-5488

Website: www.ss.ca.gov

I. ARTICLES OF INCORPORATION

A. Must provide state corporation office with the original and two typed copies of the Articles.

II. THE CORPORATE NAME

A. Name must contain corporation, incorporated, or limited or an abbreviation of the same.

B. Name must not contain words that are likely to mislead the public or contain the words bank, trust, trustee, or related words.

C. Prior to incorporation, a corporate name may be reserved for a nonrenewable period of sixty days.

D. May be filed online at the above website.

III. DIRECTORS

A. Directors need not be residents of the state or shareholders of the corporation.

B. The Articles or bylaws may prescribe additional requirements or qualifications.

C. A corporation must have three directors or more as initially stated in Articles and thereafter as many directors as stated in bylaws. However, when there are less than three shareholders, there need be only a corresponding number of directors.

D. Director(s) are normally elected at the annual meeting of shareholders.

IV. OFFICERS

A. A corporation must have a president and/or a chairman of the board, a secretary, and a chief financial officer. Other officers may be elected or appointed in accordance with provisions set forth in the bylaws.

B. The same person may hold more than one office unless provided for otherwise in the bylaws.

C. An officer performs duties stated in the bylaws, by the board of directors, or another officer to the extent consistent with the bylaws.

V. REGISTERED AGENT

A. A corporation must register an agent with the state who has an office within the state.

VI. FILING FEES

A.	Articles of Incorporation	$100.00
B.	Change of Registered Agent and Acceptance	$5.00
C.	Application for Name Reservation	$10.00
D.	Amending Articles of Incorporation	$30.00
E.	Filing Annual Report	$25.00
F.	Cost for Certified Copy of Any Document	$8.00
G.	Minimum annual franchise tax	$800.00*
H.	Expedited filing	$15.00

* Must be paid when Articles are filed, for a total of $900.00 to incorporate.

COLORADO

Title 7, Colorado Revised Statutes

> Secretary of State
> Business Division
> 1700 Broadway
> Suite 200
> Denver, CO 80290
> 303-894-2200
> Website: www.sos.state.co.us

I. ARTICLES OF INCORPORATION

    A. Must provide state corporation office with one set of original Articles, typed.

    B. Must record certificate of incorporation in each county where the corporation owns real property.

    C. May be filed online at the above website.

II. THE CORPORATE NAME

    A. Name must contain the word corporation, incorporated, company, limited, or abbreviation of the same.

    B. Prior to incorporation, a corporate name may be reserved for a period of 120 days and is renewable for another 120 days. A name search for up to three names can be done by tax for $3.00. Allow two to three business days for a response.

III. DIRECTORS

    A. Director(s) must be at least 18 years of age but need not be a resident of the state or a shareholder of the corporation.

    B. The bylaws may prescribe additional requirements or qualifications.

    C. A corporation may have as many directors as stated in bylaws.

    D. Director(s) are normally elected at the annual meeting of shareholders.

IV. OFFICERS

    A. Officers must be at least 18 years of age. Other officers may be elected or appointed in accordance with provisions set forth in the bylaws.

    B. The same person may hold more than one office.

    C. An officer performs duties stated in the bylaws or by the board of directors to the extent consistent with the bylaws.

V. REGISTERED AGENT

    A. A corporation must register an agent with the state who has an office within the state.

VI. FILING FEES

A	Articles of Incorporation	$50.00
B.	Change of Registered Agent and Acceptance	$5.00
C.	Application for Name Reservation	$50.00
D.	Amending Articles of Incorporation	$50.00
E.	Filing Annual Report	$10.00
F.	Cost for Copy of Any Document	First page free + $.50 per additional page. Certification fee $2.00

NOTE: *The fees mentioned are for online filings. Paper filings are significantly higher.*

CONNECTICUT

Chapter 601, Business Corporations—Connecticut Business Corporation Act

Secretary of State

30 Trinity Street

Hartford, CT 06106

860-509-6002 (Document Review)

Website: www.concord.sots.ct.gov

I. CERTIFICATE OF INCORPORATION

   A. Must be printed or typewritten in English.

   B. Must provide state corporation office with one copy of the Certificate.

II. THE CORPORATE NAME

   A. Name must contain the word corporation, incorporated, company, limited, Society per Azioni, or abbreviation of the same.

   B. Prior to incorporation, a corporate name may be reserved for a period of 120 days.

III. DIRECTORS

   A. Directors need not be residents of the state or shareholders of the corporation.

   B. The Certificate or bylaws may prescribe additional requirements or qualifications.

   C. A board of directors shall consist of one or more individuals with the number to be fixed in accordance with the Certificate of Incorporation or the bylaws.

   D. Director(s) are normally elected at the annual meeting of shareholders.

IV. OFFICERS

   A. A corporation shall have the offices described in its bylaws or designated by the board of directors.

   B. An officer performs duties stated in the bylaws or by the board of directors to the extent consistent with the bylaws.

V. REGISTERED AGENT

   A. Corporation must register with the state an agent at an office within the state.

VI. FILING FEES for Domestic Stock Corporations

   A. Certificate of Incorporation $50.00

   B. Change of Registered Agent and Acceptance $25.00

   C. Application for Name Reservation $30.00

   D. Amending Certificate of Incorporation $50.00

   E. Filing Annual Reports $75.00

   F. Cost for Certified Copy of Any Document $25.00

   G. Franchise tax for stock corporation $150.00 minimum

      Tax rate: One cent per share for the first 10,000 shares; plus ½ cent per share for the first 10,001–100,000 shares; plus ¼ cent per share for 100,001–1,000,000 shares; plus ⅕ cent per share for each share in excess of 1,000,000.

   H. Expedited filing available $25.00

NOTE: *The minimum fee for initial incorporation is $275.00 for the filing fee, organizational tax, and initial biennial report.*

DELAWARE

Title 8, Delaware Code
  Secretary of State
  Division of Corporations
  P..O. Box 898
  Dover, DE 19903
  302-739-3073
  Website: www.state.de.us/corp

I. CERTIFICATE OF INCORPORATION
  A. Must be printed or typewritten in English.
  B. Must provide state corporation office with the original and one exact copy of the Certificate.
  C. Must record a copy of the Certificate in the county where the registered office is located.

II. THE CORPORATE NAME
  A. Name must contain the word corporation, incorporated, association, company, club, foundation, fund, institute, society, union, syndicate, limited, or abbreviation of the same.
  B. Prior to incorporation, a corporate name may be reserved for a period of 30 days. Name may be reserved by telephone by calling 302-739-3073.

III. DIRECTORS
  A. Directors need not be residents of the state or shareholders of the corporation.
  B. The Certificate or bylaws may prescribe additional requirements or qualifications.
  C. A corporation must have one director or more as initially stated in Certificate and thereafter as many directors as stated in bylaws.
  D. Director(s) are normally elected at the annual meeting of shareholders.

IV. OFFICERS
  A. A corporation may have officers which are elected or appointed in accordance with provisions set forth in the bylaws or determined by the directors.
  B. The same person may hold more than one office unless provided for otherwise in the bylaws.
  C. An officer performs duties stated in the bylaws or by the board of directors or another officer to the extent consistent with the bylaws.
  D. One officer shall be responsible for preparing the records of any director or shareholder meeting.

V. REGISTERED AGENT
  A. A corporation must register an agent with the state who has an office within the state.

continued

VI. FILING FEES

- A. Receiving and Indexing Certificate of Incorporation $89.00
- B. Application for Name Reservation $10.00
- C. Amending Articles of Incorporation $129.00 (includes filing fee, receiving, and indexing)
- D. Filing Annual Report $20.00
- E. Cost for Certified Copy of Any Document $20.00 + $1.00 per page
- F. Incorporation Tax (for up to 1500 shares) $15.00
- G. Expedited services
  - 24 hours up to $100.00
  - same day up to $200.00
  - 2 hours $500.00

NOTE: *The minimum filing fee to initially incorporate is $50.00 for the receiving and indexing of the Certificate of Incorporation, the Incorporation Tax, and one Certified Copy.*

DISTRICT OF COLUMBIA

Title 29, District of Columbia Code

Department of Consumer and Regulatory Affairs

Corporation Division

941 North Capitol Street, N.E.

Washington, DC 20002

202-442-4400

Website: http://dcra.washingtondc.gov

I. ARTICLES OF INCORPORATION

A. Must be printed or typewritten in English.

B. Must provide Department of Consumer and Regulatory Affairs with duplicate originals.

II. THE CORPORATE NAME

A. Name must contain the word corporation, incorporated, company, limited, or abbreviation of the same.

B. Prior to incorporation, a corporate name may be reserved for a period of sixty days.

III. DIRECTORS

A. Directors need not be a shareholder of the corporation.

B. The Articles or bylaws may prescribe additional requirements or qualifications.

C. A corporation must have three directors or more as initially stated in Articles and thereafter as many directors as stated in bylaws.

D. Director(s) are normally elected at the annual meeting of shareholders.

IV. OFFICERS

A. A corporation must have a president and other officers prescribed in its bylaws.

B. The same person may hold more than one office except of president and secretary unless prohibited from doing so in the bylaws.

C. An officer performs duties stated in the bylaws, by the board of directors, or another officer to the extent consistent with the bylaws.

V. REGISTERED AGENT

A. A corporation must register an agent with the state who has an office within the district.

VI. FILING FEES

A. Articles of Incorporation	$100.00
B. Designation of Registered Agent and Acceptance	$25.00
C. Application for Name Reservation	$25.00
D. Amending Articles of Incorporation	$100.00*
E. Filing Biennial Report	$200.00
F. Cost for Certified Copy of Any Document	$5.00

* Except for changes in numbers of shares.

FLORIDA

Chapters 607 and 621, Florida Statutes

Secretary of State
Division of Corporations
P.O. Box 6327
Tallahassee, FL 32314
800-755-5111
Website: www.sunbiz.org

I. ARTICLES OF INCORPORATION
    A. Must be printed or typewritten in English.
    B. Must provide state corporation office with the original and one exact copy of the Articles.

II. THE CORPORATE NAME
    A. Name must contain the word corporation, incorporated, company, or abbreviation of the same.

III. DIRECTORS
    A. Director(s) must be a natural person, 18 years of age, but need not be a resident of the state or a shareholder of the corporation.
    B. The Articles or bylaws may prescribe additional requirements or qualifications.
    C. A corporation must have one director or more as initially stated in Articles and thereafter as many directors as stated in bylaws.
    D. Director(s) are normally elected at the annual meeting of shareholders.

IV. OFFICERS
    A. A corporation must have the officers described in its bylaws or appointed in accordance with provisions set forth in the bylaws.
    B. The same person may hold more than one office unless provided for otherwise in the bylaws.
    C. An officer performs duties stated in the bylaws or by the board of directors or another officer to the extent consistent with the bylaws.
    D. One officer shall be responsible for preparing the records of any director or shareholder meeting.

V. REGISTERED AGENT
    A. A corporation must register an agent with the state who has an office within the state.

VI. FILING FEES

A	Articles of Incorporation	$35.00
B.	Designation of Registered Agent and Acceptance	$35.00
C.	Application for Name Reservation	$35.00
D.	Amending Articles of Incorporation	$35.00
E.	Filing Annual Report	$150.00 if received before May 1
		$550.00 if received after May 1
F.	Cost for Certified Copy of Any Document	$8.75 (plus $1 per page for each page over 8, not to exceed a maximum of $52.50)

NOTE: *The minimum filing fee is $70.00 to initially incorporate includes the filing of the Articles of Incorporation and Designation of Registered Agent.*

GEORGIA

Title 14, Georgia Code
  Secretary of State
  315 West Tower
  #2 Martin Luther King, Jr. Drive
  Atlanta, GA 30334-1530
  404-656-2817
  Website: www.sos.state.ga.us/corporations

I. ARTICLES OF INCORPORATION

   A. Must be printed or typewritten in English, although name of corporation may be in another language.

   B. Must provide state corporation office with the original and one exact copy of the Articles and transmittal Form 227 (see CD-ROM).

   C. Must publish notice of intent to incorporate pursuant to Georgia law.

II. THE CORPORATE NAME

   A. Name must contain the word corporation, incorporated, company, limited, or abbreviation of the same.

   B. Prior to incorporation, a corporate name should be reserved for thirty days and the reservation may be renewed for another thirty days thereafter. This may be done on the above website or by calling 404-656-2817.

III. DIRECTORS

   A. Directors must be at least 18 years of age but need not be a resident of the state or a shareholder of the corporation.

   B. The Articles or bylaws may prescribe additional requirements or qualifications.

   C. A corporation must have one director or more as initially stated in Articles and thereafter as many directors as stated in bylaws.

   D. Director(s) are normally elected at the annual meeting of shareholders.

IV. OFFICERS

   A. A corporation must have the officers elected or appointed in accordance with provisions set forth in the bylaws.

   B. The same person may hold more than one office unless provided for otherwise in the bylaws.

   C. An officer performs duties stated in the bylaws, by the board of directors, or another officer to the extent consistent with the bylaws.

   D. One officer shall be responsible for preparing the records of any director or shareholder meeting.

V. REGISTERED AGENT

   A. A corporation must register an agent with the state who has an office within the state.

VI. FILING FEES

A. Articles of Incorporation	$100.00
B. Application for Name Reservation	$25.00
C. Amending Articles of Incorporation	$20.00
D. Filing Annual Report	$30.00

NOTE: *The fee for initially incorporating is $100.00 This includes filing the Articles of Incorporation and publishing the Notice of Intent to Incorporate—$60.00 is paid to Secretary of State and $40.00 is sent directly to, and payable to, the publisher.*

HAWAII

Title 23, Hawaii Revised Statutes

Department of Commerce and Consumer Affairs

Business Registration Division

P. O. Box 40

Honolulu, Hawaii 96810

808-586-2727

Website: www.state.hi.us/dcca/breg-seu/index.html

I. ARTICLES OF INCORPORATION

A. Must provide state corporation office with the original Articles.

B. All signatures must be in black ink.

II. THE CORPORATE NAME

A. Name must contain the word corporation, incorporated, "imited, or abbreviation of the same.

B. Prior to incorporation, a corporate name may be reserved for a period of 120 days. Name may be reserved by written application only.

III. DIRECTORS

A. The Articles or bylaws may prescribe requirements or qualifications for directors.

B. A corporation must have one director with the number be fixed in accordance with the Articles of Incorporation or the bylaws.

C. Director(s) are normally elected at the annual meeting of shareholders.

IV. OFFICERS

A. A corporation has the officers described in its bylaws or appointed by the board of directors in accordance with the bylaws.

B. The bylaws or the board of directors shall delegate to one of the officers responsibility for preparation and custody of minutes of the directors' and shareholders' meetings and for authenticating records of the corporation.

C. The same person may hold more than one office.

D. An officer performs duties stated in the bylaws, by the board of directors, or another officer to the extent consistent with the bylaws.

V. FILING FEES

A.	Articles of Incorporation	$50.00
B.	Application for Name Reservation	$10.00
C.	Amending Articles of Incorporation	$25.00
D.	Filing Annual Report	$25.00
E.	Cost for Certified Copy of Any Document	$10.00/document plus .25/page for copying
F.	Expedited Services	$50.00

IDAHO

Title 30, Idaho Code

Secretary of State

700 West Jefferson,

Basement West

Boise, ID 83720-0080

208-334-2301

Website: www.idsos.state.id.us

I. ARTICLES OF INCORPORATION

A. Must provide state corporation office with duplicate originals.

II. THE CORPORATE NAME

A. Name must contain the word corporation, incorporated, company, limited, or abbreviation of the same.

B. Prior to incorporation, a corporate name may be reserved for a period of four months.

III. DIRECTORS

A. Directors need not be residents of the state or shareholders of the corporation.

B. The Articles or bylaws may prescribe requirements or qualifications for directors.

C. A corporation must have one director with the number be fixed in accordance with the Articles of Incorporation or the bylaws.

D. Director(s) are normally elected at the annual meeting of shareholders.

IV. OFFICERS

A. A corporation has the officers described in its bylaws or appointed by the board of directors in accordance with the bylaws.

B. The bylaws or the board of directors shall delegate to one of the officers responsibility for preparation and custody of minutes of the directors' and shareholders' meetings, and for authenticating records of the corporation.

C. The same person may hold more than one office.

V. REGISTERED AGENT

A. A corporation must register an agent with the state who has an office within the state.

VI. FILING FEES

A. Articles of Incorporation

if typed (with no attachments)	$100.00
if not typed (or with attachments)	$120.00

B. Change of Registered Agent's Name/Address $20.00

C. Application for Name Reservation $20.00

D. Amending Articles of Incorporation $30.00

E. Filing Annual Report   No fee

F. Copies $.25

G. Certification $10.00

ILLINOIS

The Business Corporation Act

Secretary of State

Business Services Department

328 Howlett Building

501 South 2nd Street

Springfield, IL 62756

217-782-6961 (forms)

312-793-3380 (info—Chicago)

Website: www.sos.state.il.us/departments/business_services/home.html

I. ARTICLES OF INCORPORATION

   A. Must provide state corporation office with duplicate originals of the Articles type-written, black ink, or computer generated.

II. THE CORPORATE NAME

   A. Name must contain the word corporation, incorporated, company, limited, or abbreviation of the same.

   B. Prior to incorporation, a corporate name may be reserved for a period of ninety days.

III. DIRECTORS

   A. Directors need not be residents of the state or shareholders of the corporation.

   B. The Articles or bylaws may prescribe additional requirements or qualifications.

   C. A corporation must have one director or more as initially stated in Articles and thereafter as many directors as stated in bylaws.

   D. Director(s) are normally elected at the annual meeting of shareholders.

IV. OFFICERS

   A. A corporation must have the officers elected or appointed in accordance with provisions set forth in the bylaws.

   B. The same person may hold more than one office unless provided for otherwise in the bylaws.

   C. An officer performs duties stated in the bylaws, by the board of directors, or another officer to the extent consistent with the bylaws.

   D. One officer shall be responsible for preparing the records of any director or shareholder meeting.

V. REGISTERED AGENT

   A. A corporation must register an agent with the state who has an office within the state.

VI. FILING FEES

A. Articles of Incorporation (excluding franchise tax) $150.00

B. Designation of Registered Agent and Acceptance $5.00

C. Application for Name Reservation $25.00

D. Amending Articles of Incorporation $50.00

E. Filing Annual Report $25.00 + fee based on capital

F. Expedited Services Available $25.00 - $100.00

NOTE: *The initial franchise tax is assessed at the rate of $1.50/$1,000 on the paid-in capital represented in Illinois, with a minimum tax of $25.00. Therefore, for paid-in capital up to $16,667.00, the minimum fee for initial incorporation is $100.00.*

NOTE: *All payments must be made by certified check, cashier's check, money order, Illinois' attorney's check, or registered public accountant's check.*

INDIANA

Title 23, Indiana Statutes
> Secretary of State
> Business Services Division
> 302 West Washington Street
> Room E018
> Indianapolis, IN 46204
> 317-232-6576 or
> 317-233-3387 (fax)
> Website: www.in.gov/sos

I. ARTICLES OF INCORPORATION

    A. Must be printed or typewritten in English.

    B. Must provide state corporation office with the original and one exact copy of the Articles.

II. THE CORPORATE NAME

    A. Name must contain the word corporation, incorporated, company, limited, or abbreviation of the same.

    B. Prior to incorporation, a corporate name may be reserved for a period of 120 days. Name may be reserved only by written application.

III. DIRECTORS

    A. Directors need not be residents of the state or shareholders of the corporation.

    B. The Articles or bylaws may prescribe additional requirements or qualifications.

    C. A corporation may have one director or more as initially stated in Articles and thereafter as many directors as stated in bylaws.

    D. Director(s) are normally elected at the annual meeting of shareholders.

IV. OFFICERS

    A. A corporation must have the officers described in its Articles or bylaws, or appointed in accordance with provisions set forth in the Articles or bylaws.

    B. The same person may hold more than one office unless provided for otherwise in the bylaws.

    C. An officer performs duties stated in the bylaws, by the board of directors, or another officer to the extent consistent with the bylaws.

    D. One officer shall be responsible for preparing the records of any director or shareholder meeting.

V. REGISTERED AGENT

    A. A corporation must register an agent with the state who has an office within the state.

VI. FILING FEES

    A. Articles of Incorporation $90.00

    B. Change of Registered Agent's Name/Address   No fee

    C. Application for Name Reservation $20.00

    D. Amending Articles of Incorporation $30.00

    E. Filing Business Entity Report $30.00 every two years; $20.00 online

    F. Cost for Certified Copy of Any Document $15.00/stamp plus 1.00/page

IOWA

Chapter 490, Iowa Code

Business Services

First Floor

Lucas Building

321 East 12ᵗʰ Street

State Capitol

Des Moines, IA 50319

515-281-5204

515-242-5953 (fax)

Website: www.sos.state.ia.us

I. ARTICLES OF INCORPORATION

  A. Must be printed or typewritten in English.

  B. Must provide state corporation office with the original and one exact copy of the Articles.

  C. May be filed online at the above website.

II. THE CORPORATE NAME

  A. Name must contain the word corporation, incorporated, company, limited, or abbreviation of the same.

  B. Prior to incorporation, a corporate name may be reserved for a period of 120 days. Name may be reserved only by written application.

III. DIRECTORS

  A. Directors need not be residents of the state or shareholders of the corporation.

  B. The Articles or bylaws may prescribe additional requirements or qualifications.

  C. A corporation must have one director or more as initially stated in Articles and thereafter as many directors as stated in bylaws.

  D. Director(s) are normally elected at the annual meeting of shareholders.

IV. OFFICERS

  A. A corporation must have the officers elected or appointed in accordance with provisions set forth in the bylaws.

  B. The same person may hold more than one office unless provided for otherwise in the bylaws.

  C. An officer performs duties stated in the bylaws, by the board of directors, or another officer to the extent consistent with the bylaws.

  D. One officer shall be responsible for preparing the records of any director or shareholder meeting.

V. REGISTERED AGENT

  A.   A corporation must register an agent with the state who has an office within the state.

VI. FILING FEES
- A. Articles of Incorporation $50.00
- B. Change Registered Agent's Name/Address   No fee
- C. Application for Name Reservation $10.00
- D. Amending Articles of Incorporation $50.00
- E. Filing Biennial Report $45.00
- F. Cost for Certified Copy of Any Document $5.00/certification and 1.00/page

KANSAS

Chapter 17, Kansas Statutes
Secretary of State
Memorial Hall
120 SW 10th Street
Topeka, KS 66612-1594
785-296-4564
Website: www.kssos.org/business/business.html

I. ARTICLES OF INCORPORATION

    A. Must provide state corporation office with the original and a duplicate copy of the Articles.

II. THE CORPORATE NAME

    A. Name must contain the word corporation, incorporated, association, church, college, company, foundation, club, fund, institute, society, syndicate, limited, union, or abbreviation of the same.

    B. Prior to incorporation, a corporate name may be reserved for a period of 120 days.

III. DIRECTORS

    A. Directors need not be residents of the state or shareholders of the corporation.

    B. The Articles or bylaws may prescribe additional requirements or qualifications.

    C. A corporation must have one director or more as initially stated in Articles and thereafter as many directors as stated in bylaws.

    D. Director(s) are normally elected at the annual meeting of shareholders.

IV. OFFICERS

    A. A corporation must have the officers elected or appointed in accordance with provisions set forth in the bylaws.

    B. The same person may hold more than one office unless provided for otherwise in the bylaws.

    C. An officer performs duties stated in the bylaws or by the board of directors to the extent consistent with the bylaws.

    D. One officer shall be responsible for preparing the records of any director or shareholder meeting.

V. RESIDENT (REGISTERED) AGENT

    A. Corporation must register with the state a registered office and a resident agent at an office within the state.

VI. FILING FEES

A.	Articles of Incorporation	$90.00
B.	Change of Registered Agent or Office	$35.00
C.	Amending Articles of Incorporation (including Resignation of Resident Agent)	$20.00
D.	Filing Annual Report	$55.00
E.	Cost for Certified Copy of Any Document	$7.50 + 1.00/page

KENTUCKY

Chapter 271B, Kentucky Revised Statutes

Office of Secretary of State

P.O. Box 718

Frankfort, KY 40601

502-564-2848 (press 2 for Business filings)

502-564-7330 (press 1 for Business filings)

Website: www.sos.ky.gov/business

I. ARTICLES OF INCORPORATION

   A. Must be printed or typewritten in English.

   B. Must provide state corporation office with the original and two exact copies of the Articles. After filing, one of the exact copies shall then be filed with and recorded by the county clerk of the county in which the registered office of the corporation is located.

II. THE CORPORATE NAME

   A. Name must contain the word corporation, incorporated, company, limited, or abbreviation of the same.

   B. Prior to incorporation, a corporate name may be reserved for a period of 120 days. A name may only be reserved in writing.

III. DIRECTORS

   A. Directors need not be residents of the state or shareholders of the corporation.

   B. The Articles or bylaws may prescribe additional requirements or qualifications.

   C. A corporation must have one director or more as initially stated in Articles or bylaws, and thereafter as many directors as stated in bylaws.

   D. Director(s) are normally elected at the annual meeting of shareholders.

IV. OFFICERS

   A. A corporation shall have the officers described in the bylaws or appointed by the board of directors in accordance with provisions set forth in the bylaws.

   B. The same person may hold more than one office unless provided for otherwise in the bylaws.

   C. An officer performs duties stated in the bylaws, by the board of directors or another officer to the extent consistent with the bylaws.

   D. One officer shall be responsible for preparing the records of any director or shareholder meeting.

V. REGISTERED AGENT

   A. A corporation must register an agent with the state who has an office within the state.

continued

VI. FILING FEES

A.	Articles of Incorporation	$40.00 (plus organization tax based upon number of shares)
B.	Change Registered Agent's Name/Address	$10.00
C.	Application for Name Reservation	$20.00
D.	Amending Articles of Incorporation	$40.00
E.	Filing Annual Report	$15.00
F.	Organizational Tax (1000 shares or less)	$10.00
G.	Cost for Certified Copy of Any Document	$5.00/certificate + .50/page

NOTE: *The minimum filing fee to initially incorporate is $50.00 which includes filing the Articles of Incorporation and the organizational tax for 1,000 shares or fewer.*

LOUISIANA

Title 12, Louisiana Revised Statutes

Secretary of State

Corporations Division

P.O. Box 94125

Baton Rouge, LA 70804-9125

225-925-4704

Website: www.sec.state.la.us

I. ARTICLES OF INCORPORATION

   A. Must be printed or typewritten in English.

   B. Must provide state corporation office with the original or multiple originals of the Articles.

   C. An initial report must be filed with the Articles setting forth: 1. The name and municipal address of the corporation's registered office. 2. The full name and municipal address of each of its registered agents. 3. The names and municipal addresses, if any, of its first director(s).

II. THE CORPORATE NAME

   A. Name must contain the word corporation, incorporated, limited, company, or abbreviation of the same. If company or co. are used, it may not be preceded by the word and or an ampersand.

   B. Prior to incorporation, a corporate name may be reserved for a period of 60 days. Name may be reserved only by written application. The reservation may be extended for an additional 30 days.

III. DIRECTORS

   A. Directors need not be residents of the state or shareholders of the corporation.

   B. The Articles or bylaws may prescribe additional requirements or qualifications.

   C. A board of directors must consist of at least one natural person.

   D. Director(s) are normally elected at the annual meeting of shareholders.

IV. OFFICERS

   A. The board of directors of a corporation shall elect a president, secretary, treasurer, and may elect one or more vice presidents. Other officers may be elected or appointed in accordance with provisions set forth in the bylaws.

   B. The same person may hold more than one office unless provided for otherwise in the Articles.

   C. An officer performs duties stated in the bylaws or by the board of directors.

V. REGISTERED AGENT

   A. A corporation must register an agent with the state who has an office within the state.

continued

VI. FILING FEES

A.	Articles of Incorporation	$75.00
B.	Change of Registered Agent's Name/Address	$25.00
C.	Application for Name Reservation	$25.00
D.	Amending Articles of Incorporation	$75.00
E.	Filing Annual Report	$25.00
F.	Cost for Additional Certified Copy of Any Document	$10.00

NOTE: *The registered agent may be changed when filing the annual report without paying the $20.00 fee.*

MAINE

Title 13-A Maine Revised Statutes

Secretary of State

Bureau of Corporations, Elections, and Commissions

101 State House Station

Augusta, ME 04333

207-624-7736 (Bureau of Corporation)

Website: www.state.me.us/sos/sos.htm

I. ARTICLES OF INCORPORATION

A. Must provide state corporation office with the original Articles.

II. THE CORPORATE NAME

A. Name need not contain such words as corporation, incorporated, company, or abbreviation of the same.

B. Prior to incorporation, a corporate name may be reserved for a period of 120 days.

III. DIRECTORS

A. Directors need not be residents of the state or shareholders of the corporation.

B. The Articles or bylaws may prescribe additional requirements or qualifications.

C. A corporation must have one director or more as initially stated in Articles and thereafter as many directors as stated in bylaws.

D. Director(s) are normally elected at the annual meeting of shareholders.

IV. OFFICERS

A. A corporation must have the officers elected or appointed in accordance with provisions set forth in the bylaws.

B. The same person may hold more than one office unless provided for otherwise in the bylaws.

C. An officer performs duties stated in the bylaws, by the board of directors or another officer to the extent consistent with the bylaws.

D. One officer shall be responsible for preparing the records of any director or shareholder meeting.

V. REGISTERED CLERK AND OFFICE

A. Corporation must register with the state a clerk, who is a natural person at an office within the state.

VI. FILING FEES

A. Articles of Incorporation $145.00

B. Change of Registered Clerk and Acceptance $35.00

C. Application for Name Reservation $20.00

D. Amending Articles of Incorporation $50.00

E. Filing Annual Report $85.00

F. Cost for Certified Copy of Any Document $5.00 + $2.00/page

MARYLAND

Corporations and Associations, Title 2, Code of Maryland

State Department of Assessments and Taxation

Charter Division

301 West Preston Street

Room 801

Baltimore, MD 21201

410-767-1340

888-246-5941 (in Maryland)

Website: www.sos.state.md.us

I. ARTICLES OF INCORPORATION

    A. Must provide state corporation office with the original of the Articles, typed.

II. THE CORPORATE NAME

    A. Name must contain the word corporation, incorporated, company, limited, or abbreviation of the same.

    B. Prior to incorporation, a corporate name may be reserved by written request for a period of thirty days. Name may be checked for availability by telephone at the Department of Assessments and Taxation. If several names are being checked, the request should be made in writing.

III. DIRECTORS

    A. Directors need not be residents of the state or shareholders of the corporation.

    B. The Articles or bylaws may prescribe additional requirements or qualifications.

    C. A corporation must have one director.

    D. Director(s) are normally elected at the annual meeting of shareholders.

IV. OFFICERS

    A. A corporation must have a president, secretary, and treasurer. Other officers may be elected or appointed in accordance with provisions set forth in the bylaws.

    B. The same person may hold more than one office unless provided for otherwise in the bylaws. However, the same person may not serve as both president and vice president.

    C. An officer performs duties stated in the bylaws, by the board of directors, or another officer to the extent consistent with the bylaws.

V. RESIDENT AGENT

    A. A corporation must register an agent with the state who has an office within the state.

VI. FILING FEES

A. Articles of Incorporation	$100.00 + $20.00 minimum organization and capitalization fee	
B. Change of Resident Agent and Acceptance	$25.00	
C. Application for Name Reservation	$7.00	
D. Amending Articles of Incorporation (minimum)	$100.00	

MASSACHUSETTS

Chapter 156, Massachusetts General Laws

Secretary of the Commonwealth

Corporations Division

One Ashburton Place

17th Floor

Boston, MA 02108

617-727-9640

Website: www.state.ma.us/sec/cor/corcon.htm

I. ARTICLES OF ORGANIZATION

    A. Must provide state corporation office with the original Articles.

    B. May be filed online at the above website.

II. THE CORPORATE NAME

    A. Name must indicate that the business is a corporation by using such words as corporation, incorporated, or abbreviation of the same.

    B. Prior to incorporation, a corporate name may be reserved for a period of sixty days, which may be extended for an additional sixty days upon written request.

III. DIRECTORS

    A. Directors need not be residents of the state or shareholders of the corporation.

    B. The Articles or bylaws may prescribe additional requirements or qualifications.

    C. A corporation must have at least one director with the number being fixed in the Articles or bylaws. If the number of directors is unspecified in the Articles or bylaws, and if the corporation has more than one shareholder the number of directors shall not be less than three, unless there are only two shareholders, in which case the number of directors may be two.

    D. Director(s) are normally elected at the annual meeting of shareholders.

    E. The president must also be a director unless otherwise provided in the bylaws.

IV. OFFICERS

    A. A corporation must have a president, treasurer, and secretary. Other officers may be elected or appointed in accordance with provisions set forth in the bylaws.

    B. The same person may hold more than one office unless provided for otherwise in the bylaws.

    C. An officer performs duties stated in the bylaws, by the board of directors, or another officer to the extent consistent with the bylaws.

    D. The clerk shall be responsible for preparing the records of any director or shareholder meeting.

V. RESIDENT (REGISTERED) AGENT

    A. A corporation must register an agent with the state who has an office within the state.

continued

VI. FILING FEES

A.	Articles of Organization	$275.00 minimum
B.	Change of Registered Agent's Name/Address	$25.00; no fee if filed electronically
C.	Application for Name Reservation	$30.00
D.	Amending Articles of Incorporation	$100.00 minimum
E.	Filing Annual Report	$125.00 minimum, $100.00 if filed electronically
F.	Cost for Certified Copy of Articles	$12.00
G.	Cost for Certified Copy of Any Other Document	$7.00/first page + $2.00/additional page

MICHIGAN

Chapter 450, Michigan Compiled Laws

Michigan Department of Commerce

Corporation and Securities Bureau

Corporation Division

P.O. Box 30054

Lansing, MI 48909

517-241-6470

Website: www.michigan.gov/cis

I. ARTICLES OF INCORPORATION

A. Must be printed or typewritten in English.

B. Must provide state corporation office with the original and one exact copy of the Articles.

II. THE CORPORATE NAME

A. Name must contain the word corporation, incorporated, company, limited, or abbreviation of the same.

B. Prior to incorporation, a corporate name may be reserved for a period of six full calendar months. Two two-month extensions are also available. Name must be reserved by written application.

III. DIRECTORS

A. Directors need not be residents of the state or shareholders of the corporation.

B. The Articles or bylaws may prescribe additional requirements or qualifications.

C. A corporation must have one director or more as initially stated in Articles and thereafter as many directors as stated in bylaws.

D. Director(s) are normally elected at the annual meeting of shareholders.

IV. OFFICERS

A. A corporation must have a president, secretary, treasurer, and may have a chairman of the board, and various vice presidents. Other officers may be elected or appointed in accordance with provisions set forth in the bylaws.

B. The same person may hold more than one office unless provided for otherwise in the bylaws.

C. An officer performs duties stated in the bylaws, by the board of directors, or another officer to the extent consistent with the bylaws.

V. RESIDENT AGENT

A. Corporation must register with the state a resident agent at an office within the state.

VI. FILING FEES

A. Articles of Incorporation
(60,000 shares or less of stock) $60.00

B. Change of Registered Agent and Acceptance $5.00

C. Application for Name Reservation $10.00

D. Amending Articles of Incorporation (minimum) $10.00

E. Filing Annual Report $15.00

MINNESOTA

Chapter 302A Minnesota Statutes

> Secretary of State
> Division of Corporations
> 180 State Office Building
> 100 Rev. Martin Luther King Jr. Boulevard
> St. Paul, MN 55155-1299
> 651-296-2803
> 877-551-6767
> Website: www.sos.state.mn.us/bus.html

I. ARTICLES OF INCORPORATION

    A. Must provide state corporation office with the original Articles, typewritten or printed in black ink.

II. THE CORPORATE NAME

    A. Name must contain the word corporation, incorporated, limited, or abbreviation of the same, or the word company or its abbreviation, if it is not immediately preceded by and or an ampersand.

    B. Prior to incorporation, a corporate name may be reserved for a period of twelve months.

III. DIRECTORS

    A. Directors need not be residents of the state or shareholders of the corporation.

    B. The Articles or bylaws may prescribe additional requirements or qualifications.

    C. A corporation must have one director or more as initially stated in Articles and thereafter as many directors as stated in bylaws.

    D. Director(s) are normally elected at the annual meeting of shareholders or in manner prescribed in bylaws.

IV. OFFICERS

    A. A corporation must have a chief executive officer and a chief financial officer, however designated. Other officers may be elected or appointed in accordance with provisions set forth in the bylaws.

    B. The same person may hold more than one office unless provided for otherwise in the bylaws.

    C. An officer performs duties stated in the bylaws, by the board of directors, or another officer to the extent consistent with the bylaws.

V. REGISTERED AGENT

    A. A corporation must register an agent with the state who has an office within the state.

VI. FILING FEES

    A. Articles of Incorporation $135.00
    B. Change of Registered Agent and Acceptance   no fee
    C. Application for Name Reservation $35.00
    D. Amending Articles of Incorporation $35.00
    E. Filing Annual Report   no fee if timely filed
    F. Cost for Certified Copy of Articles $8.00
       with Amendments $11.00
    G. Expedited Services $20.00

MISSISSIPPI

Title 79, Mississippi Code

Secretary of State
Business Services Division
P.O. Box 136
Jackson, MS 39205
601-359-1633
800-256-3494
Website: www.sos.state.ms.us

I. ARTICLES OF INCORPORATION
   A. Must be printed or typewritten in English.
   B. Must provide state corporation office with the original and one exact copy of the Articles.

II. THE CORPORATE NAME
   A. Name must contain the word corporation, incorporated, company, limited, or abbreviation of the same.
   B. Prior to incorporation, a corporate name may be reserved for a period of 180 days.

III. DIRECTORS
   A. Directors need not be residents of the state or shareholders of the corporation.
   B. The Articles or bylaws may prescribe additional requirements or qualifications.
   C. The board of directors must consist of one or more individuals, initially stated in Articles and with the number specified in or fixed in accordance with the Articles or bylaws.
   D. Director(s) are normally elected at the annual meeting of shareholders.

IV. OFFICERS
   A. A corporation must have the officers described in its bylaws or appointed by the board of directors in accordance with provisions set forth in the bylaws.
   B. The same person may hold more than one office unless provided for otherwise in the bylaws.
   C. An officer performs duties stated in the bylaws, by the board of directors, or another officer to the extent consistent with the bylaws.
   D. One officer shall be responsible for preparing the records of any director or shareholder meeting.

V. REGISTERED AGENT
   A. A corporation must register an agent with the state who has an office within the state.

VI. FILING FEES
   A. Articles of Incorporation $50.00
   B. Change of Registered Agent's Name/Address $25.00
   C. Application for Name Reservation $25.00
   D. Amending Articles of Incorporation $50.00
   E. Filing Annual Report $25.00
   F. Cost for Certified Copy of Any Document $10.00/certificate + 1.00/page

MISSOURI

Chapter 351, Missouri Statutes

Secretary of State

Corporation Division

P.O. Box 778

Jefferson City, MO 65102

573-751-4153

Website: www.sos.state.mo.us

I. ARTICLES OF INCORPORATION
    A. Must be printed or typewritten in English.
    B. Must provide state corporation office with duplicate originals of the Articles.

II. THE CORPORATE NAME
    A. Name must contain the word corporation, incorporated, company, limited, or abbreviation of the same.
    B. Prior to incorporation, a corporate name may be reserved for a period of sixty days. Name availability may be checked by telephone.

III. DIRECTORS
    A. Directors need not be residents of the state or shareholders of the corporation.
    B. The Articles or bylaws may prescribe additional requirements or qualifications.
    C. A corporation must have three directors or more as initially stated in Articles and thereafter as many directors as stated in bylaws. However, when there are less than three shareholders, there need be only a corresponding number of directors.
    D. Director(s) are normally elected at the annual meeting of shareholders.

IV. OFFICERS
    A. A corporation must have a president and secretary. Other officers may be elected or appointed in accordance with provisions set forth in the bylaws.
    B. The same person may hold more than one office unless provided for otherwise in the bylaws.
    C. An officer performs duties stated in the bylaws or by the board of directors to the extent consistent with the bylaws.

V. REGISTERED AGENT
    A. A corporation must register an agent with the state who has an office within the state.

VI. FILING FEES
    A. Articles of Incorporation
        (minimum fee for up to $30,000 shares of stock)　　$58.00
    B. Change of Registered Agent's Name/Address　　$10.00
    C. Application for Name Reservation　　$25.00
    D. Amending Articles of Incorporation　　$25.00
    E. Cost for Non-Certified Copy of Any Document　　$.50/page

MONTANA

Title 35, Montana Code
   Secretary of State
   P.O. Box 202801
   Helena, MT 59620
   406-444-2034
   Website: www.sos.state.mt.us

I. ARTICLES OF INCORPORATION

   A. Must be printed or typewritten in English.

   B. Must provide state corporation office with the original and one exact copy of the Articles.

II. THE CORPORATE NAME

   A. Name must contain the word corporation, incorporated, company, limited, or abbreviation of the same.

   B. Prior to incorporation, a corporate name may be reserved for a period of 120 days.

III. DIRECTORS

   A. Directors need not be residents of the state or shareholders of the corporation.

   B. The Articles or bylaws may prescribe additional requirements or qualifications.

   C. A corporation must have one director or more as initially stated in Articles.

   D. Director(s) are normally elected at the annual meeting of shareholders.

IV. OFFICERS

   A. A corporation must have the officers described in its bylaws or as appointed by the board of directors in accordance with the bylaws.

   B. The same person may hold more than one office.

   C. An officer performs duties stated in the bylaws, by the board of directors, or another officer to the extent consistent with the bylaws.

V. REGISTERED AGENT

   A. A corporation must register an agent with the state who has an office within the state.

VI. FILING FEES

A.	Articles of Incorporation	$70.00*
B.	Change of Registered Agent's Name/Address	No fee
C.	Application for Name Reservation	$10.00
D.	Amending Articles of Incorporation	$15.00
E.	Filing Annual Report	$15.00
F.	Cost for Certified Copy of Any Document	$10.00

* At the time of incorporation, a domestic corporation must pay $20.00 and a license fee. The minimum charge to incorporate is $70.00. This fee will give the corporation the authority to issue up to $50,000 worth of shares.

NEBRASKA

Chapter 21, Revised Nebraska Statutes

Secretary of State

P.O. Box 94608

Lincoln, NE 68509-4608

402-471-4079

402-471-3666 (fax)

Website: www.sos.state.ne.us/business/corp_serv

I. ARTICLES OF INCORPORATION

    A. Must be printed or typewritten in English.

    B. Must provide state corporation office with the original and one exact copy of the Articles.

II. THE CORPORATE NAME

    A. Name must contain the word corporation, incorporated, company, limited, or abbreviation of the same.

    B. Prior to incorporation, a corporate name may be reserved for a period of 120 days.

III. DIRECTORS

    A. Directors need not be residents of the state or shareholders of the corporation.

    B. The Articles or bylaws may prescribe additional requirements or qualifications.

    C. A corporation must have one director or more as initially stated in bylaws.

    D. Director(s) are normally elected at the annual meeting of shareholders.

IV. OFFICERS

    A. A corporation must have the offices as described in the bylaws or as appointed by the board of directors in accordance with the bylaws.

    B. The same person may hold more than one office.

    C. An officer performs duties stated in the bylaws or by the board of directors to the extent consistent with the bylaws.

V. REGISTERED AGENT

    A. A corporation must register an agent with the state who has an office within the state.

VI. FILING FEES

    A. Articles of Incorporation $60.00 + $5.00 per page
       (not over $10,000.00 of capital stock)

    B. Change of Registered Agent's Name/Address $25.00 + $5.00 per page

    C. Application for Name Reservation $25.00 + $5.00 per page

    D. Amending Articles of Incorporation $25.00 + $5.00 per page

    E. Cost for Certified Copy of Any Document $10.00 + $1.00 per page

NEVADA

Chapter 78, Nevada Revised Statutes
Secretary of State
202 North Carson Street
Carson City, NV 89701
775-684-5708
Website: www.sos.state.nv.us/comm_rec/index.htm

I. ARTICLES OF INCORPORATION

   A. Must provide state corporation office with the original and one exact copy of the Articles, typed or written in black ink.

II. THE CORPORATE NAME

   A. Any name which appears to be that of a natural person must contain the word corporation, incorporated, company, limited, or abbreviation of the same, or any other word that identifies the name as not being that of a natural person.

   B. Prior to incorporation, a corporate name may be reserved for a period of ninety days.

III. DIRECTORS

   A. Directors need not be residents of the state or shareholders of the corporation.

   B. The Articles or bylaws may prescribe additional requirements or qualifications.

   C. A corporation must have one director or more as initially stated in Articles and thereafter as many directors as stated in bylaws.

   D. Director(s) are normally elected at the annual meeting of shareholders.

IV. OFFICERS

   A. A corporation must have a president, secretary, and treasurer. Other officers may be elected or appointed in accordance with provisions set forth in the bylaws.

   B. The same person may hold more than one office unless provided for otherwise in the bylaws.

   C. An officer performs duties stated in the bylaws or by the board of directors to the extent consistent with the bylaws.

V. REGISTERED AGENT

   A. A corporation must register an agent with the state who has a street address within the state.

VI. FILING FEES

   A. Articles of Incorporation ($75,000 or less of capital stock) $75.00

   B. Change of Registered Agent's Name/Address $60.00

   C. Application for Name Reservation $25.00

   D. Amending Articles of Incorporation $175.00 (minimum fee)

   E. Filing Annual Report $125.00

   F. Cost for Certified Copy of Articles when a copy is provided $30.00

NEW HAMPSHIRE

Chapter 293-A, New Hampshire Business Corporation Act

Corporation Division
Department of State
107 North Main Street
Concord, NH 03301
603-271-3246
Website: www.sos.nh.gov/corporate/index.html

I. ARTICLES OF INCORPORATION
   A. Must be printed or typewritten in black ink.
   B. Must provide state corporation office with the original and one exact copy of the Articles.

II. THE CORPORATE NAME
   A. Name must contain the word corporation, incorporated, limited, or abbreviation of the same.
   B. Prior to incorporation, a corporate name may be reserved for a period of 120 days.

III. DIRECTORS
   A. Directors need not be residents of the state or shareholders of the corporation.
   B. The Articles or bylaws may prescribe additional requirements or qualifications.
   C. A corporation must have one director or more as initially stated in bylaws.
   D. Director(s) are normally elected at the annual meeting of shareholders.

IV. OFFICERS
   A. A corporation must have the officers described in its bylaws or as appointed by the board of directors in accordance with the bylaws.
   B. The same person may hold more than one office.
   C. An officer performs duties stated in the bylaws or by the board of directors to the extent consistent with the bylaws.

V. REGISTERED AGENT
   A. A corporation must register an agent with the state who has an office within the state.

VI. FILING FEES
   A. Articles of Incorporation $100.00
   B. Change of Registered Agent's Name/Address $15.00
   C. Application for Name Reservation $15.00
   D. Amending Articles of Incorporation $35.00
   E. Cost for Certified Copy of Any Document $5.00 + $1.00 per page
   F. Annual Report $100.00

NEW JERSEY

Title 14A, New Jersey Revised Statutes

Department of Treasury

Division of Corporate Filing

P.O. Box 308

Trenton, NJ 08625-0308

609-292-1730

609-984-6681 (fax)

Website: www.state.nj.us/treasury/revenue/index.html

I. CERTIFICATE OF INCORPORATION

   A. Must be printed or typewritten in English.

   B. Must provide state corporation office with the original and one exact copy of the Certificate.

II. THE CORPORATE NAME

   A. Name must contain the word corporation, incorporated, company, abbreviation of the same, or ltd.

   B. Prior to incorporation, most corporate names may be reserved for a period of 120 days. Name must be reserved through written application.

III. DIRECTORS

   A. Directors need not be residents of the state or shareholders of the corporation, but must be at least 18 years of age.

   B. The Certificate or bylaws may prescribe additional requirements or qualifications.

   C. A corporation must have one director or more as initially stated in Certificate and thereafter as many directors as stated in bylaws.

   D. Director(s) are normally elected at the annual meeting of shareholders.

IV. OFFICERS

   A. A corporation must have a president, secretary, and treasurer. Other officers may be elected.

   B. The same person may hold more than one office unless provided for otherwise in the bylaws.

   C. An officer performs duties stated in the bylaws or by the board of directors to the extent consistent with the bylaws.

V. REGISTERED AGENT

   A. A corporation must register an agent with the state who has a street address within the state.

VI. FILING FEES

   A. Certificate of Incorporation $125.00
   B. Change of Registered Agent's Name/Address $25.00
   C. Application for Name Reservation $50.00
   D. Amending Certificate of Incorporation $75.00
   E. Filing Annual Report $50.00

NEW MEXICO

Chapter 53, New Mexico Statutes

Public Regulation Commission

Corporation Department

P.O. Box 1269

Santa Fe, NM 87504-1269

505-827-4502

505-827-4508

800-947-4722 (New Mexico Residents only)

505-827-4387 (fax)

Website: www.nmprc.state.nm.us/corporations/corpshome.htm

I. ARTICLES OF INCORPORATION

    A. Must provide state corporation office with an original and one copy of the Articles.

II. THE CORPORATE NAME

    A. Name must contain the word corporation, incorporated, company, limited, or abbreviation of the same.

    B. Prior to incorporation, a corporate name may be reserved for a period of 120 days.

III. DIRECTORS

    A. Directors need not be residents of the state or shareholders of the corporation.

    B. The Articles or bylaws may prescribe additional requirements or qualifications.

    C. A corporation must have one director or more as initially stated in Articles and thereafter as many directors as stated in bylaws.

    D. Director(s) are normally elected at the annual meeting of shareholders.

IV. OFFICERS

    A. A corporation must have the officers described in its bylaws or appointed in accordance with provisions set forth in the bylaws.

    B. The same person may hold more than one office unless provided for otherwise in the bylaws.

    C. An officer performs duties stated in the bylaws or by the board of directors to the extent consistent with the bylaws.

    D. One officer shall be responsible for preparing the records of any director or shareholder meeting.

V. REGISTERED AGENT

    A. A corporation must register an agent with the state who has an office within the state.

VI. FILING FEES

    A. Articles of Incorporation (up to $100,000.00 capital stock) $100.00

    B. Change of Registered Agent's Name/Address $25.00

    C. Application for Name Reservation $25.00

    D. Amending Articles of Incorporation $100.00

    E. Filing Annual Report $25.00

    F. Cost for Certified Copy of Any Document $10.00 (minimum)

    G. Cost for Certified Copy of Articles $25.00 + $1.00 per page

NEW YORK

Chapter 4, Consolidated Laws of New York

    Department of State

    Division of Corporations and State Records

    41 State Street

    Albany, NY 12231

    518-473-2492

    518-474-1418 (fax)

    Website: www.dos.state.ny.us

I. CERTIFICATE OF INCORPORATION

    A. Must be printed or typewritten in English.

    B. Must provide state corporation office with the original Certificate. State sends certified copy to county where corporation is to be located.

II. THE CORPORATE NAME

    A. Name must contain the word corporation, incorporated, limited, or abbreviation of the same. The name cannot include the following words and phrases: board of trade, chamber of commerce, community renewal, state police, state trooper, tenant relocation, urban development, urban relocation, acceptance, annuity, assurance, bank, benefit, bond, casualty, doctor, endowment, fidelity, finance, guaranty, indemnity, insurance, investment, lawyer, loan, mortgage, savings, surety, title, trust, or underwriter.

    B. Prior to incorporation, a corporate name may be reserved for a period of sixty days. Name must be reserved through written application and can be renewed upon written request twice for a period of sixty days each.

III. DIRECTORS

    A. Directors need not be residents of the state or shareholders of the corporation, but must be at least 18 years of age.

    B. The Certificate or bylaws may prescribe additional requirements or qualifications.

    C. A corporation must have one director or more as initially stated in Certificate and thereafter as many directors as stated in bylaws.

    D. Director(s) are normally elected at the annual meeting of shareholders.

IV. OFFICERS

    A. A corporation may have such officers as may be elected or appointed in accordance with provisions set forth in the bylaws.

    B. The same person may hold more than one office.

    C. An officer performs duties stated in the bylaws, by the board of directors, or shareholders to the extent consistent with the bylaws.

V. REGISTERED AGENT

    A. The Secretary of State must be designated as agent for the corporation to accept service of process. The corporation may also register an agent with the state who has a residential street address or an office within the state.

VI. FILING FEES

A. Certificate of Incorporation $135.00*

B. Certificate of Change of Registered Agent's Name/Address $30.00

C. Application for Name Reservation $20.00

D. Amending Certificate of Incorporation $60.00

E. Cost for Certified Copy of Any Document $10.00

*This fee includes a minimum tax of $10.00 for issuance of up to 200 shares of no par value stock. The tax will be higher if more shares are issued.

NORTH CAROLINA

Chapter 55, General Statutes of North Carolina

Department of Secretary of State

Corporations Division

P.O. Box 29622

Raleigh, NC 27626-0622

919-807-2225

919-807-2039 (fax)

Website: www.secretary.state.nc.us/corporations

I. ARTICLES OF INCORPORATION

   A. Must be printed or typewritten in English.

   B. Must provide state corporation office with the original and one exact copy of the Articles.

II. THE CORPORATE NAME

   A. Name must contain the word corporation, incorporated, company, limited, or abbreviation of the same.

   B. Prior to incorporation, a corporate name may be reserved for a period of 120 days.

III. DIRECTORS

   A. Directors need not be residents of the state or shareholders of the corporation.

   B. The Articles or bylaws may prescribe additional requirements or qualifications.

   C. A corporation must have one director or more as initially stated in Articles.

   D. Director(s) are normally elected at the annual meeting of shareholders.

IV. OFFICERS

   A. A corporation must have the officers as provided in accordance with provisions set forth in the bylaws.

   B. The same person may hold more than one office unless provided for otherwise in the bylaws. No one person may act in more than one capacity where an action by two or more officers is required.

   C. An officer performs duties stated in the bylaws, by the board of directors, or another officer to the extent consistent with the bylaws.

   D. One officer shall be responsible for maintaining and authenticating the records of the corporations.

V. REGISTERED AGENT

   A. Corporation must register an agent with the state who has an office with a street address within the state.

VI. FILING FEES

   A. Articles of Incorporation $125.00
   B. Change of Registered Agent's Name/Address $5.00
   C. Application for Name Reservation $30.00
   D. Amending Articles of Incorporation $50.00
   E. Filing Annual Report $20.00
   F. Cost for Certified Copy of Any Document $5.00 + $1.00 per page

NORTH DAKOTA

Title 10, North Dakota Century Code

Secretary of State

Capitol Building

600 East Boulevard Avenue

Department 108

Bismarck, ND 58505

701-328-2910

800-297-5124

Website: www.state.nd.us/sec

I. ARTICLES OF INCORPORATION

   A. Must be in English.

   B. Must provide state corporation office with the original of the Articles.

II. THE CORPORATE NAME

   A. Name must contain the word corporation, incorporated, company, limited, or abbreviation of the same.

   B. Prior to incorporation, a corporate name may be reserved for a period of twelve months.

III. DIRECTORS

   A. Directors need not be residents of the state or shareholders of the corporation.

   B. The Articles or bylaws may prescribe additional requirements or qualifications.

   C. A corporation must have one director or more as initially stated in Articles and thereafter as many directors as stated in bylaws.

   D. Director(s) are normally elected at the annual meeting of shareholders unless there is a fixed term as prescribed in the bylaws.

IV. OFFICERS

   A. A corporation must have a president, one or more vice presidents, a secretary, and a treasurer. Other officers may be elected or appointed in accordance with provisions set forth in the bylaws.

   B. The same person may hold more than one office unless provided for otherwise in the bylaws.

   C. An officer performs duties stated in the bylaws or by the board of directors to the extent consistent with the bylaws.

   D. One officer shall be responsible for preparing the records of any director or shareholder meeting.

V. REGISTERED AGENT

   A. A corporation must register an agent with the state who has an office within the state and provide the state with his or her Social Security number or federal ID number.

continued

VI. FILING FEES

A.	Articles of Incorporation	$30.00*
B.	Designation of Registered Agent	$10.00
C.	License Fee (first $50,000 of stock)	$50.00
D.	Application for Name Reservation	$10.00
E.	Amending Articles of Incorporation	$20.00
F.	Filing Annual Report	$25.00
G.	Cost for Certified Copy of Any Document	$15.00 + $1.00/4 pgs

* A minimum of $90.00 is required to incorporate. This includes the filing fee, license fee, and designation of registered agent.

OHIO

Title 17, Ohio Revised Statutes

Secretary of State

Business Services Division

180 East Broad Street

16th Floor

Columbus, OH 43215

614-466-3910

877-767-6446

Website: www.state.oh.us/sos

I. ARTICLES OF INCORPORATION

   A. Must provide state corporation office with the original and one exact copy of the Articles.

II. THE CORPORATE NAME

   A. Name must contain the word corporation, incorporated, company, or abbreviation of the same.

   B. Prior to incorporation, a corporate name may be reserved for a period of 180 days. Name must be reserved through written application and payment of fee. Name availability may be checked over the telephone.

III. DIRECTORS

   A. Directors need not be residents of the state or shareholders of the corporation.

   B. The Articles or bylaws may prescribe additional requirements or qualifications.

   C. A corporation must have three directors or more as initially stated in Articles and thereafter as many directors as stated in bylaws. However, when there are less than three shareholders, there need be only a corresponding number of directors.

   D. Director(s) are normally elected at the annual meeting of shareholders.

IV. OFFICERS

   A. A corporation must have a president, secretary, and treasurer. Other officers may be elected by the board of directors.

   B. The same person may hold more than one office unless provided for otherwise in the bylaws.

   C. An officer performs duties as determined by the board of directors.

V. REGISTERED AGENT

   A. A corporation must register a statutory agent with the state who has a street address within the state.

continued

VI. FILING FEES

A. Articles of Incorporation (minimum fee) $125.00

   10¢ per share,   1–1000
   5¢ per share,   1001–10,000
   2¢ per share,   10,001–50,000
   1¢ per share,   50,001–100,000
   ½¢ per share,   100,001–500,000
   ¼¢ per share over 500,000

B. Change of Registered Agent's Name/Address $25.00

C. Application for Name Reservation $50.00

D. Amending Articles of Incorporation $50.00

E. Biennial Report $25.00

F. Cost for Certified Copy of Any Document $5.00 + $1.00 per page

OKLAHOMA

Title 18, Oklahoma Statutes

    Secretary of State

    Corporation Division

    2300 North Lincoln Boulevard

    Room 101

    Oklahoma City, OK 73105-4897

    405-521-3912

    405-521-3771 (fax)

    Website: www.sos.state.ok.us

I. CERTIFICATE OF INCORPORATION

    A. Must provide state corporation office with the original and one conformed copy of the Certificate.

II. THE CORPORATE NAME

    A. Name must contain the word association, club, corporation, incorporated, company, fund, foundation, institute, society, union, syndicate, limited, or abbreviation of the same.

    B. Prior to incorporation, a corporate name may be reserved for a period of sixty days. Name must be reserved through written application, but informal name check may be done over the telephone at 405-521-3912.

III. DIRECTORS

    A. Directors need not be residents of the state or shareholders of the corporation.

    B. The Certificate or bylaws may prescribe additional requirements or qualifications.

    C. A corporation must have one director or more as initially stated in the bylaws unless the number of directors is fixed by the Certificate.

    D. Director(s) are normally elected at the annual meeting of shareholders.

IV. OFFICERS

    A. A corporation must have the offices as provided for by the bylaws.

    B. The same person may hold more than one office unless provided for otherwise in the bylaws.

    C. An officer performs duties stated in the bylaws or by the board of directors to the extent consistent with the bylaws.

V. REGISTERED AGENT

    A. A corporation must register an agent with the state who has an office within the state.

VI. FILING FEES

A. Certificate of Incorporation (minimum)	$50.00
B. Change of Registered Agent's Name/Address	$25.00
C. Application for Name Reservation	$10.00
D. Amending Certificate of Incorporation	$50.00
E. Cost for Certified Copy of Any Document	$10.00 + $1.00 per page

OREGON

Title 7, Oregon Revised Statutes

Corporation Division

Secretary of State

255 Capitol Street, N.E.

Suite 151

Salem, OR 97310-1327

503-986-2200

503-378-4381 (fax)

Website: www.filinginOregon.com

I. ARTICLES OF INCORPORATION

A. Must be printed or typewritten in English.

B. Must provide state corporation office with the original Articles. Articles need not be typed or printed, but must be legible.

II. THE CORPORATE NAME

A. Name must contain the word corporation, incorporated, company, limited, or abbreviation of the same.

B. Prior to incorporation, a corporate name may be reserved for a period of 120 days. Name must be reserved through written application.

III. DIRECTORS

A. Directors need not be residents of the state or shareholders of the corporation.

B. The Articles or bylaws may prescribe additional requirements or qualifications.

C. A corporation must have one director or more as initially stated in Articles.

D. Director(s) are normally elected at the annual meeting of shareholders.

IV. OFFICERS

A. A corporation must have a president and secretary. Other officers may be elected or appointed in accordance with provisions set forth in the bylaws.

B. The same person may hold more than one office unless provided for otherwise in the bylaws.

C. An officer performs duties stated in the bylaws, by the board of directors, or another officer to the extent consistent with the bylaws.

D. The secretary shall be responsible for preparing the records of any director or shareholder meeting.

V. REGISTERED AGENT

A. A corporation must register an agent with the state who has an office within the state.

VI. FILING FEES

A. Articles of Incorporation	$50.00
B. Change of Registered Agent's Name/Address	no fee
C. Application for Name Reservation	$50.00
D. Amending Articles of Incorporation	$50.00
E. Filing Annual Report	$20.00
F. Cost for Certified Copy of Any Document	$15.00

PENNSYLVANIA

Title 19, Pennsylvania Statutes

Department of State

Corporation Bureau

P.O. Box 8722

Harrisburg, PA 17120

717-787-1057

888-659-9962

Website: www.dos.state.pa.us

I. ARTICLES OF INCORPORATION
   A. Printed or typewritten is preferred.
   B. Must provide state corporation office with the original copy of the Articles, along with docking statement.

II. THE CORPORATE NAME
   A. Name must contain the word corporation, incorporated, company, limited, or an abbreviation thereof, or association, fund, or syndicate, if appropriate.
   B. Prior to incorporation, a corporate name may be reserved for a period of 120 days. Name must be reserved through written or faxed application, accompanied by docketing statement.

III. DIRECTORS
   A. Directors need not be a resident of the commonwealth or a shareholder of the corporation.
   B. The Articles or bylaws may prescribe additional requirements or qualifications.
   C. A corporation must have one director or more as initially stated in Articles and thereafter as many directors as stated in bylaws.
   D. Director(s) are normally elected at the annual meeting of shareholders.

IV. OFFICERS
   A. A corporation must have a president, secretary, and treasurer. Other officers may be elected or appointed in accordance with provisions set forth in the bylaws.
   B. The same person may hold more than one office unless provided for otherwise in the bylaws.
   C. An officer performs duties stated in the bylaws or by the board of directors to the extent consistent with the bylaws.

V. REGISTERED AGENT
   A. Corporation need not have a registered agent, but must register with the state an office located in the state which can accept service of process.

VI. FILING FEES
   A. Articles of Incorporation $125.00
   B. Change of Registered Agent's Name/Address $70.00
   C. Application for Name Reservation $70.00
   D. Amending Articles of Incorporation $70.00
   E. Cost for Certified Copy of Any Document $55.00 fee + $3.00/page

RHODE ISLAND

Title 7, General Laws of Rhode Island, Ch 7-1.2

Secretary of State

Corporations Division

100 North Main Street

1st Floor

Providence, RI 02903

401-222-3040

Website: www3.sec.state.ri.us/divs/corps/index.html

I. ARTICLES OF INCORPORATION
   A. Must provide state corporation office with the original and one exact copy of the Articles.

II. CORPORATE NAME
   A. Name must contain the word corporation, incorporated, company, limited, or abbreviation of the same.
   B. Prior to incorporation, a corporate name may be reserved for a period of 120 days. Name availability may be requested over the telephone but may only be reserved through written application.

III. DIRECTORS
   A. Directors need not be residents of the state or shareholders of the corporation.
   B. The Articles or bylaws may prescribe additional requirements or qualifications.
   C. A corporation may have one or more members as initially stated in Articles and thereafter as many directors as stated in bylaws.
   D. Director(s) are normally elected at the annual meeting of shareholders.

IV. OFFICERS
   A. A corporation must have a president, secretary, and treasurer. Other officers may be elected or appointed in accordance with provisions set forth in the bylaws.
   B. The same person may hold more than one office unless provided for otherwise in the bylaws.
   C. An officer performs duties stated in the bylaws or by the board of directors to the extent consistent with the bylaws.

V. REGISTERED AGENT
   A. A corporation must register an agent with the state who has a physical address within the state.

VI. FILING FEES
   A. Articles of Incorporation $230.00
   B. Change of Registered Agent's Name/Address $20.00
   C. Application for Name Reservation $50.00
   D. Amending Articles of Incorporation $70.00
   E. Filing Annual Report $50.00
   F. Cost for Certified Copy of Any Document $10.00 + .15 per page

SOUTH CAROLINA

Title 33, Code of Laws of South Carolina

Secretary of State

Division of Corporations

P.O. Box 11350

Columbia, SC 29211

803-734-2158

Website: www.scsos.com/corporations.htm

I. ARTICLES OF INCORPORATION

    A. Must be printed or typewritten in English.

    B. Must provide state corporation office with the original copy of the Articles, in black ink. The Articles must be signed by an incorporator, accompanied by a certificate stating that the requirements have been complied with and that the corporation is organized for a lawful and proper purpose, signed by an attorney licensed in South Carolina.

II. THE CORPORATE NAME

    A. Name must contain the word corporation, incorporated, company, limited, or abbreviation of the same.

    B. Prior to incorporation, a corporate name may be reserved for a period of 120 days. Name must be reserved through written application.

III. DIRECTORS

    A. Directors need not be residents of the state or shareholders of the corporation.

    B. The Articles or bylaws may prescribe additional requirements or qualifications.

    C. A corporation must have one director or more as initially stated in Articles.

    D. Director(s) are normally elected at the annual meeting of shareholders.

IV. OFFICERS

    A. A corporation must have the offices as described in the bylaws or as appointed by the board of directors in accordance with the bylaws.

    B. The same person may hold more than one office unless provided for otherwise in the bylaws.

    C. An officer performs duties stated in the bylaws, by the board of directors, or another officer to the extent consistent with the bylaws.

    D. One officer shall be responsible for preparing the records of any director or shareholder meeting.

V. REGISTERED AGENT

    A. A corporation must register an agent with the state who has an office within the state.

continued

VI. FILING FEES

A. Articles of Incorporation — $135.00
B. Change of Registered Agent's Name/Address — $10.00
C. Application for Name Reservation — $10.00
D. Amending Articles of Incorporation — $110.00
E. Filing Annual Report — $25.00
F. Cost for Certified Copy of Any Document — $3.00 + $.50/page

SOUTH DAKOTA

Title 47, South Dakota Codified Laws

    Secretary of State

    State Capitol

    500 East Capitol Avenue

    Suite 204

    Pierre, SD 57501

    605-773-4845

    Website: www.sdsos.gov

I. ARTICLES OF INCORPORATION

    A. Must provide state corporation office with the original and one exact copy of the Articles.

    B. Corporation cannot start business until the value of at least $1,000 has been received for the issuance of shares.

II. THE CORPORATE NAME

    A. Name must contain the word corporation, incorporated, company, limited, or abbreviation of the same.

    B. Prior to incorporation, a corporate name may be reserved for a period of 120 days. Name must be reserved through written application.

III. DIRECTORS

    A. Directors need not be residents of the state or shareholders of the corporation.

    B. The Articles or bylaws may prescribe additional requirements or qualifications.

    C. A corporation must have one director or more as initially stated in Articles and thereafter as many directors as stated in bylaws.

    D. Director(s) are normally elected at the annual meeting of shareholders.

IV. OFFICERS

    A. A corporation shall have the officers described in its bylaws or appointed by the board in accordance with provisions set forth in the bylaws.

    B. The same person may hold more than one office unless provided for otherwise in the bylaws.

    C. An officer performs duties stated in the bylaws, by the board of directors, or another officer to the extent consistent with the bylaws.

V. REGISTERED AGENT

    A. A corporation must register an agent with the state who has an office within the state.

VI. FILING FEES

A. Articles of Incorporation	$125.00
B. Change of Registered Agent's Name/Address	$10.00
C. Application for Name Reservation	$20.00
D. Amending Articles of Incorporation	$50.00
E. Filing Annual Report	$30.00
F. Cost for Certified Copy of Any Document	$10.00 + $1.00/page

TENNESSEE

Title 48, Tennessee Code
  Department of State
  Division of Business Services
  312 Eighth Avenue North
  6th Floor
  Nashville, TN 37243
  615-741-2286
  Website: www.tennessee.gov/sos/bus_svc/corporations.htm

I.   CHARTER

  A. Must provide state corporation office with the original of the Charter typewritten or printed in English.

II. THE CORPORATE NAME

  A. Name must contain the word corporation, incorporated, company, or abbreviation of the same.

  B. Prior to incorporation, a corporate name may be reserved for a period of four months. Name must be reserved through written application. A preliminary check may be done via telephone at 615-741-2286.

III. DIRECTORS

  A. Directors need not be residents of the state or shareholders of the corporation.

  B. The Charter or bylaws may prescribe additional requirements or qualifications.

  C. A corporation must have one director or more as initially stated in Charter and thereafter as many directors as stated in bylaws.

  D. Director(s) are normally elected at the first annual meeting of shareholders and at each annual meeting thereafter.

IV. OFFICERS

  A. A corporation must have a president and secretary. Other officers may be elected or appointed in accordance with provisions set forth in the bylaws.

  B. The same person may hold more than one office unless provided for otherwise in the bylaws.

  C. An officer performs duties stated in the bylaws, by the board of directors, or another officer to the extent consistent with the bylaws.

  D. One officer shall be responsible for preparing the records of any director or shareholder meeting.

V.   REGISTERED AGENT

  A. A corporation must register an agent with the state who has an office within the state.

VI. FILING FEES

A.	Charter	$100.00
B.	Application for Name Reservation	$20.00
C.	Amending Charter	$20.00
D.	Filing Annual Report	$20.00
E.	Cost for Certified Copy of Any Document	$20.00
F.	Change of Registered Agent	$20.00

TEXAS

Business Corporation Act of Texas, Texas Civil Statutes

Secretary of State

Corporation Division

P.O. Box 13697

Austin, TX 78711

512-463-5555

Website: www.sos.state.tx.us

I. ARTICLES OF INCORPORATION

    A. Must provide state corporation office with the original and one exact copy of the Articles.

II. THE CORPORATE NAME

    A. Name must contain the word corporation, incorporated, company, or abbreviation of the same.

    B. Prior to incorporation, a corporate name may be reserved for a period of 120 days. Name availability may be checked over the telephone, but must be reserved through written application.

III. DIRECTORS

    A. Directors need not be residents of the state or shareholders of the corporation.

    B. The Articles or bylaws may prescribe additional requirements or qualifications.

    C. A corporation must have one director or more as initially stated in Articles and thereafter as many directors as stated in bylaws.

    D. Director(s) are normally elected at the annual meeting of shareholders.

IV. OFFICERS

    A. A corporation must have a president and secretary. Other officers may be elected or appointed in accordance with provisions set forth in the bylaws.

    B. The same person may hold more than one office unless provided for otherwise in the bylaws.

    C. An officer performs duties stated in the bylaws, by the board of directors, or another officer to the extent consistent with the bylaws.

    D. One officer shall be responsible for preparing the records of any director or shareholder meeting.

V. REGISTERED AGENT

    A. A corporation must register an agent with the state who has an office within the state.

VI. FILING FEES

    A. Articles of Incorporation $300.00

    B. Change Registered Agent Address $15.00

    C. Application for Name Reservation $40.00

    D. Amending Articles of Incorporation $150.00

    E. Expedited Processing $25.00 (per document)

UTAH

Title 16, Utah Code

Department of Commerce
Division of Corporations and Commercial Code
P.O. Box 146705
160 East 300 South
Salt Lake City, UT 84114-6705
801-530-4849
877-526-3994
801-530-6438 (fax)
Website: www.commerce.utah.gov/cor/index.htm

I. ARTICLES OF INCORPORATION
    A. Must provide state corporation office with the original and one exact copy of the Articles.

II. THE CORPORATE NAME
    A. Name must contain the word corporation, incorporated, company, or abbreviation of the same.
    B. Prior to incorporation, a corporate name may be reserved for a period of 120 days.

III. DIRECTORS
    A. Directors need not be residents of the state or shareholders of the corporation.
    B. The Articles or bylaws may prescribe additional requirements or qualifications.
    C. A corporation must have three directors or more as initially stated in Articles and thereafter as many directors as stated in bylaws.
    D. Director(s) are normally elected at the annual meeting of shareholders.

IV. OFFICERS
    A. A corporation must have at least one officer. Other officers may be elected or appointed in accordance with provisions set forth in the bylaws. The same individual may hold more than one office.
    B. The same person may hold more than one office in the corporation.
    C. An officer performs duties stated in the bylaws or by the board of directors to the extent consistent with the bylaws.
    D. One officer shall be responsible for preparing the records of any director or shareholder meeting.

V. REGISTERED AGENT
    A. A corporation must register an agent with the state who has an office within the state.

VI. FILING FEES
    A. Articles of Incorporation $52.00
    B. Application for Name Reservation $22.00
    C. Amending Articles of Incorporation $37.00
    D. Filing Annual Report $12.00
    E. Cost for Certified Copy of Any Document $12.00 + $.30/page
    F. Expedited Services $75.00

VERMONT

Title 11A, Vermont Statutes
   Secretary of State
   Division of Corporations
   81 River Street
   Montpelier, VT 05609-1104
   802-828-2386
   802-828-2853 (fax)
   Website: www.sec.state.vt.us/corps/corpindex.htm

I. ARTICLES OF incorporation
   A. Must be printed or typewritten in English.
   B. Must provide state corporation office with the original and one exact copy of the Article

II. THE CORPORATE NAME
   A. Name must contain the word corporation, incorporated, company, limited, or abbrev
      tion of the same.
   B. Prior to incorporation, a corporate name may be reserved for a period of 120 day
      Name must be reserved through written application.

III. DIRECTORS
   A. Directors need not be residents of the state or shareholders of the corporation.
   B. The Articles or bylaws may prescribe additional requirements or qualifications.
   C. A corporation must have three directors or more as initially stated in Articles a
      thereafter as many directors as stated in bylaws. However, when there are less th
      three shareholders, there need be only a corresponding number of directors.
   D. Director(s) are normally elected at the annual meeting of shareholders.

IV. OFFICERS
   A. A corporation must have a president and a secretary. Other officers may be elected
      appointed in accordance with provisions set forth in the bylaws.
   B. The same person may hold more than one office except the offices of president and se
      retary.
   C. An officer performs duties as determined by the board of directors.
   D. One officer shall be responsible for preparing the records of any director or sharehold
      meeting.

V. REGISTERED AGENT
   A. A corporation must register an agent with the state who has an office within the state.

VI. FILING FEES
   A. Articles of Incorporation $75.00
   B. Change of Registered Agent's Name/Address $20.00
   C. Application for Name Reservation $20.00
   D. Amending Articles of Incorporation $25.00
   E. Filing Annual Report $25.00
   F. Cost for Certified Copy of Any Document $1.00 per page

VIRGINIA

Title 13.1, Code of Virginia

State Corporation Commission

P.O. Box 1197

Richmond, VA 23218

804-371-9967

800-552-7945

Website: www.state.va.us/scc

I. ARTICLES OF INCORPORATION

    A. Must be printed or typewritten in English.

    B. Must provide state corporation office with the original and one exact copy of the Articles.

II. THE CORPORATE NAME

    A. Name must contain the word corporation, incorporated, company, limited, or abbreviation of the same.

    B. Prior to incorporation, a corporate name may be reserved for a period of 120 days. Name availability may be checked by telephone but may only be reserved by written application.

III. DIRECTORS

    A. Directors need not be a resident of the commonwealth or a shareholder of the corporation.

    B. The Articles or bylaws may prescribe additional requirements or qualifications.

    C. A corporation must have one director or more as initially stated in Articles and thereafter as many directors as stated in bylaws.

    D. Director(s) are normally elected at the annual meeting of shareholders.

IV. OFFICERS

    A. A corporation must have the officers elected or appointed in accordance with the provisions set forth in the bylaws.

    B. The same person may hold more than one office unless provided for otherwise in the bylaws.

    C. An officer performs duties stated in the bylaws or by the board of directors or another officer to the extent consistent with the bylaws.

V. REGISTERED AGENT

    A. A corporation must register an agent with the state who has an office within the state.

continued

VI. FILING FEES
- A. Articles of Incorporation $75.00
  (up to 25,000 shares of capital stock)
- B. Change of Registered Agent's Name/Address   no fee
- C. Application for Name Reservation $10.00
- D. Amending Articles of Incorporation $25.00
- E. Filing Annual Report   no charge
- F. Annual Registration Fee $100.00
  (5,000 and below shares of stock
- G. Cost for Certified Copy of Any Document $1.00/page + $3.00/certificate

WASHINGTON

Title 23B, Revised Code of Washington
   Secretary of State
   Corporation Division
   P.O. Box 40234
   Olympia, WA 98504-0234
   360-753-7115
   Website: www.secstate.wa.gov/corps

I. ARTICLES OF INCORPORATION
   A. Must be printed or typewritten in English.
   B. Must provide state corporation office with the original and one exact copy of the Articles.

II. THE CORPORATE NAME
   A. Name must contain the word corporation, incorporated, company, limited, or abbreviation of the same.
   B. Prior to incorporation, a corporate name may be reserved for a period of 180 days.

III. DIRECTORS
   A. Directors need not be residents of the state or shareholders of the corporation.
   B. The Articles or bylaws may prescribe additional requirements or qualifications.
   C. A corporation must have one director or more with the number specified in or fixed in accordance with the Articles or bylaws.
   D. Director(s) are normally elected at the annual meeting of shareholders.

IV. OFFICERS
   A. A corporation must have the officers elected or appointed in accordance with provisions set forth in the bylaws.
   B. The same person may hold more than one office unless provided for otherwise in the bylaws.
   C. An officer performs duties as stated in the bylaws, by the board of directors, or another officer to the extent consistent with the bylaws.

V. REGISTERED AGENT
   A. A corporation must register an agent with the state who has an office within the state.

VI. FILING FEES

A. Articles of Incorporation	$175.00
B. Change of Registered Agent/Office	$10.00
C. Application for Name Reservation	$30.00
D. Amending Articles of Incorporation	$30.00
E. Filing Annual Report	$10.00
F. Cost for Certified Copy of Any Document	$10.00/certificate and .20/page
G. Annual License Fee	$59.00
H. Expedited Service	$20.00

WEST VIRGINIA

Chapter 31, West Virginia Code

Secretary of State
Corporations Division
State Capitol
Building 1
Suite 157-K
Charleston, WV 25305
304-558-8000
Website: www.wvsos.com

I. ARTICLES OF INCORPORATION
   A. Must provide state corporation office with duplicate originals of the Articles.

II. THE CORPORATE NAME
   A. Name must contain the word corporation, incorporated, company, limited, or abbreviation of the same.
   B. Prior to incorporation, a corporate name may be reserved for a period of 120 days by written application. A corporate name may be reserved temporarily by telephone or in person for a period of seven (7) days.

III. DIRECTORS
   A. Directors need not be residents of the state or shareholders of the corporation.
   B. The Articles or bylaws may prescribe additional requirements or qualifications.
   C. A corporation may have one director or more as initially stated in Articles or bylaws.
   D. Director(s) are normally elected at the annual meeting of shareholders.

IV. OFFICERS
   A. A corporation must have a president, secretary and treasurer. Other officers may be elected or appointed in accordance with provisions set forth in the bylaws.
   B. The same person may hold more than one office, except those of president and secretary.
   C. An officer performs duties as stated in the bylaws or by the board of directors to the extent consistent with the bylaws.

V. REGISTERED AGENT
   A. Secretary of State accepts process for each corporation and will mail process on to the corporation.

VI. FILING FEES

A. Articles of Incorporation — approximately $100.00, depending on time of year and amount of stock

B. Change of Name of Officer — $15.00

C. Application for Name Reservation — $15.00

D. Amending Articles of Incorporation — $25.00
(plus any increase in license tax)

E. Filing Annual Report — $10.00
(plus license tax and attorney-in-fact fee)

F. Cost for Certified Copy of Any Document — $15.00

WISCONSIN

Chapter 180, Wisconsin Statutes

Department of Financial Institutions

Division of Corporate and Consumer Services

Corporate Section

P.O. Box 7846

Madison, WI 53707

608-261-7577

608-267-6813 (fax)

Website: www.wdfi.org/corporations

I. ARTICLES OF INCORPORATION

   A. Articles must be written in English.

   B. Must provide state corporation office with the original and one exact copy of the Articles.

II. THE CORPORATE NAME

   A. Name must contain the word corporation, incorporated, company, limited, or abbreviation of the same.

   B. Prior to incorporation, a corporate name may be reserved for a period of 120 days. Name may be reserved through written application or by telephone for an extra fee.

III. DIRECTORS

   A. Directors need not be residents of the state or shareholders of the corporation.

   B. The Articles or bylaws may prescribe additional requirements or qualifications.

   C. A corporation must have one director or more as initially stated in Articles or bylaws.

   D. Director(s) are normally elected at the annual meeting of shareholders.

IV. OFFICERS

   A. A corporation must have the officers as elected or appointed in accordance with provisions set forth in the bylaws.

   B. The same person may hold more than one office unless provided for otherwise in the bylaws.

   C. An officer performs duties stated in the bylaws, by the board of directors, or another officer to the extent consistent with the bylaws.

V. REGISTERED AGENT

   A. A corporation must register an agent with the state who has an office within the state.

VI. FILING FEES

   A. Articles of Incorporation $100.00

      (up to 9,000 shares for minimum fee)

   B. Change of Registered Agent's Name/Address $10.00

   C. Application for Name Reservation $15.00

   D. Telephone Application for Name Reservation $30.00

   E. Amending Articles of Incorporation $40.00

      (plus $.01 for each additional share created)

   F. Filing Annual Report $25.00 electronic

                                     $40.00 paper

   G. Cost for Certified Copy of Any Document $5.00 + $.50/page

   H. Expedited Service $25.00

WYOMING

Title 17, Wyoming Statutes

Secretary of State

State Capitol Building

Room 110

200 West 24th Street

Cheyenne, WY 82002

307-777-7311

3070777-5339 (fax)

Website: http://soswy.state.wy.us/corporat/corporat.htm

I. ARTICLES OF INCORPORATION
    A. Articles must be written in English.
    B. Must provide state corporation office with the original and one exact copy of the Articles.

II. THE CORPORATE NAME
    A. Name may not contain language stating or implying that the corporation is organized for an unlawful purpose.
    B. Prior to incorporation, a corporate name may be reserved for a period of 120 days. Name availability may be checked over the telephone, but must be reserved through written application.

III. DIRECTORS
    A. Directors need not be residents of the state or shareholders of the corporation.
    B. The Articles or bylaws may prescribe additional requirements or qualifications.
    C. A corporation may have one director or more as initially specified in or fixed in accordance with the Articles or bylaws.
    D. Director(s) are normally elected at the annual meeting of shareholders.

IV. OFFICERS
    A. A corporation has the officers as elected or appointed in accordance with provisions set forth in the bylaws.
    B. The same person may hold more than one office unless provided for otherwise in the bylaws.
    C. An officer performs duties stated in the bylaws, by the board of directors, or another officer to the extent consistent with the bylaws.
    D. One officer shall be responsible for preparing the records of any director or shareholder meeting.

V. REGISTERED AGENT
    A. A corporation must register an agent with the state who has an office within the state.
    B. Written consent of the registered agent must accompany filing.

VI. FILING FEES

    A. Articles of Incorporation $100.00

    B. Change of Registered Agent's Name/Address $20.00

    C. Application for Name Reservation $50.00

    D. Amending Articles of Incorporation $50.00

    E. Filing Annual Report $25.00*

    F. Cost for Certified Copy of Any Document $.50**

* To renew registered agent plus minimum of $50.00 Annual Report License Tax.

** $.50 for the first 10 pages + $.15 for every page thereafter + $3.00 certification.

State Incorporation Forms

Many states have created a template form for preparing and filing your Articles of Incorporation. For each state that has done so, we have included the state form on the attached CD-ROM, and made each form able to be filled in so you can prepare your form directly on your computer. (Some states prevent modification of their form to make it fillable and must be done either on their website or using a typewriter.)

You do not have to use the state form and may want to include different information from what it asks. However, you must be sure to include everything your state requires of you as discussed throughout this book.

This appendix includes template forms of **ARTICLES OF INCORPORATION** you can use in place of your state's form or when your state does not provide a separate form.

Forms A through F are the forms that must be filed with the Secretary of State or corporation division to form a corporation.

Form A applies to the following states:

Alabama	Kansas	Ohio
Alaska†	Kentucky	Oregon
Arizona	Maryland	Pennsylvania
Arkansas	Michigan	Rhode Island
California	Minnesota	South Carolina
Colorado	Mississippi	Texas*
District of Columbia	Missouri	Utah*
Florida	Montana	Vermont
Georgia	Nebraska	Virginia‡
Idaho	Nevada	Washington
Illinois	New Hampshire	West Virginia
Indiana	New Mexico	Wisconsin
Iowa	North Carolina	Wyoming
	North Dakota	

* For Texas and Utah, the document must state: "The corporation will not commence business until $1,000 has been received for issuance of stock." (can be paid in money, labor, or property)

† For Alaska, the document must state: "The name and address of each alien affiliate is: (if none, please indicate N/A)"

---

    name   complete resident or business address

‡ For Virginia, the document must state that the registered agent is either (1) a resident of Virginia and either a director of the corporation or a member of the Virginia Bar Association or (2) a professional corporation or professional limited liability company registered under Section 54.1-3902.

Form B applies to the following states:
Louisiana
Tennessee

Form C applies to the following states:
Connecticut
Delaware
New Jersey
New York
Oklahoma

Form D applies to the following states:
Maine
Massachusetts

Form E applies to the following state:
South Dakota

Form F applies to the following state:
Hawaii

STATE OF _____

ARTICLES OF INCORPORATION
OF

_____,
A BUSINESS/STOCK CORPORATION

The name of the corporation is _____.

The business and mailing address of the corporation is _____
_____.
[street address, city, county, state, zip]

The duration of the corporation is perpetual.

The corporation has been organized to transact any and all lawful business for which corporations may be incorporated in this state.

The aggregate number of shares which the corporation shall have the authority to issue is _____ and the par value of each shall be _____. (typically "no par value")

The number of directors constituting the initial board of directors of the corporation is _____, and their names and addresses are:

The location and street address of the initial registered office is _____
_____ (must be located within the state) (list county also) and the name of its initial registered agent at such address is
_____.

The name and address of each incorporator:

In witness thereof, the undersigned incorporator(s) have executed these articles of incorporation this _____ day of _____, _____.

_____   _____
Witness   Incorporator

_____   _____
Witness   Incorporator

State of _____
County of _____

On _____, the above person(s) appeared before me, a notary public and are personally known or proved to me to be the person(s) whose name(s) is/are subscribed to the above instrument who acknowledged that he/she executed the instrument.

                                    _____
                                    Notary

(Notary stamp or seal)
This document prepared by:

This page intentionally blank.

STATE OF
_____

ARTICLES OF INCORPORATION
OF
_____,
A BUSINESS/STOCK CORPORATION

The name of the corporation is _____.

The business and mailing address of the corporation is _____
_____.
[street address, city, county, state, zip]

The duration of the corporation is perpetual.

The corporation has been organized to transact any and all lawful business for which corporations may be incorporated in this state.

The aggregate number of shares which the corporation shall have the authority to issue is _____ and the par value of each shall be _____. (typically "no par value")

The location and street address of the initial registered office is _____
_____ (must be located within the state) (list county also) and the name of its initial registered agent at such address is _____.

The corporation's federal tax identification number is _____

The name and address of each incorporator:

In witness thereof, the undersigned incorporator(s) have executed these articles of incorporation this _____ day of _____, _____.

_____   _____
Witness   Incorporator

_____   _____
Witness   Incorporator

_____   _____
Witness   Incorporator

State of _____
County of _____

On _____, the above person(s) appeared before me, a notary public and are personally known or proved to me to be the person(s) whose name(s) is/are subscribed to the above instrument who acknowledged that he/she executed the instrument.

                                           _____
                                           Notary

(Notary stamp or seal)
This document prepared by:

This page intentionally blank.

STATE OF
_____

ARTICLES OF INCORPORATION
OF
_____,
A BUSINESS/STOCK CORPORATION

The name of the corporation is _____.

The business and mailing address of the corporation is _____
_____.
[street address, city, county, state, zip]

The duration of the corporation is perpetual.

The corporation has been organized to transact any and all lawful business for which corporations may be incorporated in this state.

The aggregate number of shares which the corporation shall have the authority to issue is _____ and the par value of each shall be _____. (typically "no par value")

The amount of the total authorized capitalized stock of this corporation is _____ dollars ($_____) divided into _____ shares, of _____ dollars ($_____).

The number of directors constituting the initial board of directors of the corporation is _____, and their names and addresses are:

The location and street address of the initial registered office is _____
_____ (must be located within the state) (list county also) and the name of its initial registered agent at such address is _____
_____.

The name and address of each incorporator:

In witness thereof, the undersigned incorporator(s) have executed these articles of incorporation this _____ day of _____, _____.

_____
Incorporator

_____
Incorporator

State of _____
County of _____

On _____, the above person(s) appeared before me, a notary public and are personally known or proved to me to be the person(s) whose name(s) is/are subscribed to the above instrument who acknowledged that he/she executed the instrument.

_____
Notary

(Notary stamp or seal)
This document prepared by:

This page intentionally blank.

STATE OF
_____

ARTICLES OF INCORPORATION
OF
_____,

A BUSINESS/STOCK CORPORATION

The name of the corporation is _____.

The business and mailing address of the corporation is _____
_____.
[street address, city, county, state, zip]

The duration of the corporation is perpetual.

The corporation has been organized to transact any and all lawful business for which corporations may be incorporated in this state.

The aggregate number of shares which the corporation shall have the authority to issue is _____ and the par value of each shall be _____. (typically "no par value")

The number of directors constituting the initial board of directors of the corporation is ____ and their names and addresses are:
_____
_____

The location and street address of the initial registered office is _____
_____ (must be located within the state) (list county also) and the name of its initial registered agent at such address is _____.

The fiscal year shall be _____.

The name and address of each officer:

Title	Name	Address
PRESIDENT	_____	
TREASURER	_____	
CLERK	_____	

The name and address of each incorporator:

In witness thereof, the undersigned incorporator(s) have executed these articles of incorporation this _____ day of _____, _____.

_____
Incorporator

_____
Incorporator

State of _____
County of _____

On _____, the above person(s) appeared before me, a notary public and are personally known or proved to me to be the person(s) whose name(s) is/are subscribed to the above instrument who acknowledged that he/she executed the instrument.

_____
Notary

(Notary stamp or seal)
This document prepared by:

This page intentionally blank.

STATE OF
_____

ARTICLES OF INCORPORATION
OF
_____,
A BUSINESS/STOCK CORPORATION

The name of the corporation is _____.

The business and mailing address of the corporation is _____
_____.
[street address, city, county, state, zip]

The corporation has been organized to transact any and all lawful business for which corporations may be incorporated in this state.

The names of the initial subscribers for shares, the number of shares subscribed for, the subscription price and the amount of capital paid are as follows:

Name of initial subscribers:
1. _____
2. _____
3. _____

Number of shares subscribed for by each corresponding subscriber:
1. _____
2. _____
3. _____

Subscription price for the shares subscribed for by each subscriber:
1. _____
2. _____
3. _____

Amount of capital paid in cash by each subscriber:
1. _____
2. _____
3. _____

The name and address of each incorporator:
_____
_____.

In witness thereof, the undersigned incorporator(s) have executed these articles of incorporation this _____ day of _____, _____.

_____
Incorporator

_____
Incorporator

State of _____
County of _____

On _____, the above person(s) appeared before me, a notary public and are personally known or proved to me to be the person(s) whose name(s) is/are subscribed to the above instrument who acknowledged that he/she executed the instrument.

_____
Notary

(Notary stamp or seal)
This document prepared by:

This page intentionally blank.

STATE OF
_____

ARTICLES OF INCORPORATION
OF

_____,

A BUSINESS/STOCK CORPORATION

The name of the corporation is _____.

The business and mailing address of the corporation is _____
_____.

[street address, city, county, state, zip]

The duration of the corporation is perpetual.

The corporation has been organized to transact any and all lawful business for which corporations may be incorporated in this state.

The aggregate number of shares which the corporation shall have the authority to issue is _____ and the par value of each shall be _____. (typically "no par value")

The corporation will not commence business until consideration of the value of at least one thousand dollars ($1,000.00) has been received for the issuance of shares.

The number of directors constituting the initial board of directors of the corporation is _____, and their names and addresses are:

The location and street address of the initial registered office is _____
_____ (must be located within the state)
(list county also) and the name of its initial registered agent at such address is _____
_____.

The corporation's federal tax identification number is _____.

The fiscal year shall be _____.

The name and address of each officer:
<u>Title</u>   <u>Name</u>   <u>Address</u>

The name and address of each incorporator:
_____
_____

In witness thereof, the undersigned incorporator(s) have executed these articles of incorporation this _____ day of _____, _____.

_____
Incorporator

_____
Incorporator

State of _____

County of _____

On _____, the above person(s) appeared before me, a notary public and are personally known or proved to me to be the person(s) whose name(s) is/are subscribed to the above instrument who acknowledged that he/she executed the instrument.

_____
Notary

[Notary stamp or seal]

This document prepared by:

_____

Consent of Appointment by the Registered Agent

I, _____, hereby give my consent to serve as the registered agent for _____

    [name of registered agent]

_____.

                   [corporate name]

Dated _____, _____.

_____
[signature of registered agent]

Articles prepared by:

Corporate Forms

appendix c

This Appendix contains the blank forms you can use in forming and running your corporation. These forms, as well as state-specific forms, can be found on the CD-ROM.

_____   [date]

_____
_____
_____
_____

Dear Sir or Madam:

Enclosed please find the necessary documents for the corporate registration of
_____, along with a check in the
amount of $_____ for the filing fee and any other required costs.

Also enclosed are photocopies of the corporate documents. Please return them to me
with the filing date stamped on them.

Thank you,

_____

This page intentionally blank.

Form **SS-4**
(Rev. December 2001)
Department of the Treasury
Internal Revenue Service

Application for Employer Identification Number

(For use by employers, corporations, partnerships, trusts, estates, churches, government agencies, Indian tribal entities, certain individuals, and others.)

▶ See separate instructions for each line.   ▶ Keep a copy for your records.

EIN

OMB No. 1545-0003

Type or print clearly.

1 Legal name of entity (or individual) for whom the EIN is being requested

2 Trade name of business (if different from name on line 1)

3 Executor, trustee, "care of" name

4a Mailing address (room, apt., suite no. and street, or P.O. box)

5a Street address (if different) (Do not enter a P.O. box.)

4b City, state, and ZIP code

5b City, state, and ZIP code

6 County and state where principal business is located

7a Name of principal officer, general partner, grantor, owner, or trustor

7b SSN, ITIN, or EIN

8a **Type of entity** (check only one box)

- ☐ Sole proprietor (SSN) _____
- ☐ Partnership
- ☐ Corporation (enter form number to be filed) ▶ _____
- ☐ Personal service corp.
- ☐ Church or church-controlled organization
- ☐ Other nonprofit organization (specify) ▶ _____
- ☐ Other (specify) ▶

- ☐ Estate (SSN of decedent) _____
- ☐ Plan administrator (SSN) _____
- ☐ Trust (SSN of grantor) _____
- ☐ National Guard ☐ State/local government
- ☐ Farmers' cooperative ☐ Federal government/military
- ☐ REMIC ☐ Indian tribal governments/enterprises
- Group Exemption Number (GEN) ▶ _____

8b If a corporation, name the state or foreign country (if applicable) where incorporated

State

Foreign country

9 **Reason for applying** (check only one box)

- ☐ Started new business (specify type) ▶ _____
- ☐ Hired employees (Check the box and see line 12.)
- ☐ Compliance with IRS withholding regulations
- ☐ Other (specify) ▶

- ☐ Banking purpose (specify purpose) ▶ _____
- ☐ Changed type of organization (specify new type) ▶ _____
- ☐ Purchased going business
- ☐ Created a trust (specify type) ▶ _____
- ☐ Created a pension plan (specify type) ▶ _____

10 Date business started or acquired (month, day, year)

11 Closing month of accounting year

12 First date wages or annuities were paid or will be paid (month, day, year). **Note:** *If applicant is a withholding agent, enter date income will first be paid to nonresident alien. (month, day, year)* . . . . ▶

13 Highest number of employees expected in the next 12 months. **Note:** *If the applicant does not expect to have any employees during the period, enter "-0-."* . . . . ▶

Agricultural	Household	Other

14 Check **one** box that best describes the principal activity of your business.

- ☐ Construction ☐ Rental & leasing ☐ Transportation & warehousing
- ☐ Real estate ☐ Manufacturing ☐ Finance & insurance
- ☐ Health care & social assistance ☐ Wholesale–agent/broker
- ☐ Accommodation & food service ☐ Wholesale–other ☐ Retail
- ☐ Other (specify)

15 Indicate principal line of merchandise sold; specific construction work done; products produced; or services provided.

16a Has the applicant ever applied for an employer identification number for this or any other business? . . . . ☐ Yes ☐ No
Note: *If "Yes," please complete lines 16b and 16c.*

16b If you checked "Yes" on line 16a, give applicant's legal name and trade name shown on prior application if different from line 1 or 2 above.
Legal name ▶   Trade name ▶

16c Approximate date when, and city and state where, the application was filed. Enter previous employer identification number if known.
Approximate date when filed (mo., day, year)   City and state where filed   Previous EIN

Third Party Designee

Complete this section **only** if you want to authorize the named individual to receive the entity's EIN and answer questions about the completion of this form.

Designee's name

Designee's telephone number (include area code)
( )

Address and ZIP code

Designee's fax number (include area code)
( )

Under penalties of perjury, I declare that I have examined this application, and to the best of my knowledge and belief, it is true, correct, and complete.

Applicant's telephone number (include area code)
( )

Name and title (type or print clearly) ▶

Applicant's fax number (include area code)
( )

Signature ▶   Date ▶

For Privacy Act and Paperwork Reduction Act Notice, see separate instructions.   Cat. No. 16055N   Form **SS-4** (Rev. 12-2001)

Do I Need an EIN?

File Form SS-4 if the applicant entity does not already have an EIN but is required to show an EIN on any return, statement, or other document.[1] **See also the separate instructions for each line on Form SS-4.**

IF the applicant...	AND...	THEN...
Started a new business	Does not currently have (nor expect to have) employees	Complete lines 1, 2, 4a–6, 8a, and 9–16c.
Hired (or will hire) employees, including household employees	Does not already have an EIN	Complete lines 1, 2, 4a–6, 7a–b (if applicable), 8a, 8b (if applicable), and 9–16c.
Opened a bank account	Needs an EIN for banking purposes only	Complete lines 1–5b, 7a–b (if applicable), 8a, 9, and 16a–c.
Changed type of organization	Either the legal character of the organization or its ownership changed (e.g., you incorporate a sole proprietorship or form a partnership)[2]	Complete lines 1–16c (as applicable).
Purchased a going business[3]	Does not already have an EIN	Complete lines 1–16c (as applicable).
Created a trust	The trust is other than a grantor trust or an IRA trust[4]	Complete lines 1–16c (as applicable).
Created a pension plan as a plan administrator[5]	Needs an EIN for reporting purposes	Complete lines 1, 2, 4a–6, 8a, 9, and 16a–c.
Is a foreign person needing an EIN to comply with IRS withholding regulations	Needs an EIN to complete a Form W-8 (other than Form W-8ECI), avoid withholding on portfolio assets, or claim tax treaty benefits[6]	Complete lines 1–5b, 7a–b (SSN or ITIN optional), 8a–9, and 16a–c.
Is administering an estate	Needs an EIN to report estate income on Form 1041	Complete lines 1, 3, 4a–b, 8a, 9, and 16a–c.
Is a withholding agent for taxes on non-wage income paid to an alien (i.e., individual, corporation, or partnership, etc.)	Is an agent, broker, fiduciary, manager, tenant, or spouse who is required to file **Form 1042,** Annual Withholding Tax Return for U.S. Source Income of Foreign Persons	Complete lines 1, 2, 3 (if applicable), 4a–5b, 7a–b (if applicable), 8a, 9, and 16a–c.
Is a state or local agency	Serves as a tax reporting agent for public assistance recipients under Rev. Proc. 80-4, 1980-1 C.B. 581[7]	Complete lines 1, 2, 4a–5b, 8a, 9, and 16a–c.
Is a single-member LLC	Needs an EIN to file **Form 8832,** Classification Election, for filing employment tax returns, **or** for state reporting purposes[8]	Complete lines 1–16c (as applicable).
Is an S corporation	Needs an EIN to file **Form 2553,** Election by a Small Business Corporation[9]	Complete lines 1–16c (as applicable).

[1] For example, a sole proprietorship or self-employed farmer who establishes a qualified retirement plan, or is required to file excise, employment, alcohol, tobacco, or firearms returns, must have an EIN. **A partnership, corporation, REMIC (real estate mortgage investment conduit), nonprofit organization (church, club, etc.), or farmers' cooperative must use an EIN for any tax-related purpose even if the entity does not have employees.**

[2] However, **do not** apply for a new EIN if the existing entity only **(a)** changed its business name, **(b)** elected on Form 8832 to change the way it is taxed (or is covered by the default rules), or **(c)** terminated its partnership status because at least 50% of the total interests in partnership capital and profits were sold or exchanged within a 12-month period. (The EIN of the terminated partnership should continue to be used. See Regulations section 301.6109-1(d)(2)(iii).)

[3] Do not use the EIN of the prior business unless you became the "owner" of a corporation by acquiring its stock.

[4] However, IRA trusts that are required to file **Form 990-T,** Exempt Organization Business Income Tax Return, must have an EIN.

[5] A plan administrator is the person or group of persons specified as the administrator by the instrument under which the plan is operated.

[6] Entities applying to be a Qualified Intermediary (QI) need a QI-EIN even if they already have an EIN. **See Rev. Proc. 2000-12.**

[7] See also *Household employer* on page 4. (**Note:** State or local agencies may need an EIN for other reasons, e.g., hired employees.)

[8] Most LLCs **do not** need to file Form 8832. See **Limited liability company (LLC)** on page 4 for details on completing Form SS-4 for an LLC.

[9] An existing corporation that is electing or revoking S corporation status should use its previously-assigned EIN.

Instructions for Form SS-4
(Rev. September 2003)

 **Department of the Treasury**
Internal Revenue Service

For use with Form SS-4 (Rev. December 2001)
Application for Employer Identification Number.
Section references are to the Internal Revenue Code unless otherwise noted.

General Instructions

Use these instructions to complete **Form SS-4,**
Application for Employer Identification Number. Also see
Do I Need an EIN? on page 2 of Form SS-4.

Purpose of Form

Use Form SS-4 to apply for an employer identification
number (EIN). An EIN is a nine-digit number (for
example, 12-3456789) assigned to sole proprietors,
corporations, partnerships, estates, trusts, and other
entities for tax filing and reporting purposes. The
information you provide on this form will establish your
business tax account.

 *An EIN is for use in connection with your
business activities only. Do **not** use your EIN in
place of your social security number (SSN).*

Items To Note

Apply online. You can now apply for and receive an EIN
online using the internet. See **How To Apply** below.

File only one Form SS-4. Generally, a sole proprietor
should file only one Form SS-4 and needs only one EIN,
regardless of the number of businesses operated as a
sole proprietorship or trade names under which a
business operates. However, if the proprietorship
incorporates or enters into a partnership, a new EIN is
required. Also, each corporation in an affiliated group
must have its own EIN.

EIN applied for, but not received. If you do not have an
EIN by the time a return is due, write "Applied For" and
the date you applied in the space shown for the number.
Do not show your SSN as an EIN on returns.

If you do not have an EIN by the time a tax deposit is
due, send your payment to the Internal Revenue Service
Center for your filing area as shown in the instructions for
the form that you are filing. Make your check or money
order payable to the "United States Treasury" and show
your name (as shown on Form SS-4), address, type of
tax, period covered, and date you applied for an EIN.

How To Apply

You can apply for an EIN online, by telephone, by fax, or
by mail depending on how soon you need to use the EIN.
Use only one method for each entity so you do not
receive more than one EIN for an entity.

Online. You can receive your EIN by internet and use it
immediately to file a return or make a payment. Go to the

IRS website at **www.irs.gov/businesses** and click on
Employer ID Numbers under **topics.**

Telephone. You can receive your EIN by telephone and
use it immediately to file a return or make a payment.
Call the IRS at **1-800-829-4933.** (International applicants
must call 215-516-6999.) The hours of operation are 7:00
a.m. to 10:00 p.m. The person making the call must be
authorized to sign the form or be an authorized designee.
See **Signature** and **Third Party Designee** on page 6.
Also see the **TIP** below.

If you are applying by telephone, it will be helpful to
complete Form SS-4 before contacting the IRS. An IRS
representative will use the information from the Form
SS-4 to establish your account and assign you an EIN.
Write the number you are given on the upper right corner
of the form and sign and date it. Keep this copy for your
records.

If requested by an IRS representative, mail or fax
(facsimile) the signed Form SS-4 (including any Third
Party Designee authorization) within 24 hours to the IRS
address provided by the IRS representative.

 *Taxpayer representatives can apply for an EIN
on behalf of their client and request that the
EIN be faxed to their **client** on the same day.
Note: By using this procedure, you are
authorizing the IRS to fax the EIN without a cover sheet.*

Fax. Under the Fax-TIN program, you can receive your
EIN by fax within 4 business days. Complete and fax
Form SS-4 to the IRS using the Fax-TIN number listed on
page 2 for your state. A long-distance charge to callers
outside of the local calling area will apply. Fax-TIN
numbers can only be used to apply for an EIN. **The
numbers may change without notice.** Fax-TIN is
available 24 hours a day, 7 days a week.

Be sure to provide your fax number so the IRS can fax
the EIN back to you. **Note:** By using this procedure, you
are authorizing the IRS to fax the EIN without a cover
sheet.

Mail. Complete Form SS-4 at least 4 to 5 weeks before
you will need an EIN. Sign and date the application and
mail it to the service center address for your state. You
will receive your EIN in the mail in approximately 4
weeks. See also **Third Party Designee** on page 6.

**Call 1-800-829-4933 to verify a number or to ask
about the status of an application by mail.**

Cat. No. 62736F

Where To Fax or File

If your principal business, office or agency, or legal residence in the case of an individual, is located in:	Call the Fax-TIN number shown or file with the "Internal Revenue Service Center" at:
Connecticut, Delaware, District of Columbia, Florida, Georgia, Maine, Maryland, Massachusetts, New Hampshire, New Jersey, New York, North Carolina, Ohio, Pennsylvania, Rhode Island, South Carolina, Vermont, Virginia, West Virginia	Attn: EIN Operation P. 0. Box 9003 Holtsville, NY 11742-9003 Fax-TIN 631-447-8960
Illinois, Indiana, Kentucky, Michigan	Attn: EIN Operation Cincinnati, OH 45999 Fax-TIN 859-669-5760
Alabama, Alaska, Arizona, Arkansas, California, Colorado, Hawaii, Idaho, Iowa, Kansas, Louisiana, Minnesota, Mississippi, Missouri, Montana, Nebraska, Nevada, New Mexico, North Dakota, Oklahoma, Oregon, Puerto Rico, South Dakota, Tennessee, Texas, Utah, Washington, Wisconsin, Wyoming	Attn: EIN Operation Philadelphia, PA 19255 Fax-TIN 215-516-3990
If you have no legal residence, principal place of business, or principal office or agency in any state:	Attn: EIN Operation Philadelphia, PA 19255 Telephone 215-516-6999 Fax-TIN 215-516-3990

How To Get Forms and Publications

Phone. You can order forms, instructions, and publications by phone 24 hours a day, 7 days a week. Call 1-800-TAX-FORM (1-800-829-3676). You should receive your order or notification of its status within 10 workdays.

Personal computer. With your personal computer and modem, you can get the forms and information you need using the IRS website at **www.irs.gov** or File Transfer Protocol at **ftp.irs.gov.**

CD-ROM. For small businesses, return preparers, or others who may frequently need tax forms or publications, a CD-ROM containing over 2,000 tax products (including many prior year forms) can be purchased from the National Technical Information Service (NTIS).

To order **Pub. 1796,** Federal Tax Products on CD-ROM, call **1-877-CDFORMS** (1-877-233-6767) toll free or connect to **www.irs.gov/cdorders.**

Tax Help for Your Business

IRS-sponsored Small Business Workshops provide information about your Federal and state tax obligations.

For information about workshops in your area, call 1-800-829-4933.

Related Forms and Publications

The following **forms** and **instructions** may be useful to filers of Form SS-4:
- **Form 990-T,** Exempt Organization Business Income Tax Return
- **Instructions for Form 990-T**
- **Schedule C (Form 1040),** Profit or Loss From Business
- **Schedule F (Form 1040),** Profit or Loss From Farming
- **Instructions for Form 1041 and Schedules A, B, D, G, I, J, and K-1,** U.S. Income Tax Return for Estates and Trusts
- **Form 1042,** Annual Withholding Tax Return for U.S. Source Income of Foreign Persons
- **Instructions for Form 1065,** U.S. Return of Partnership Income
- **Instructions for Form 1066,** U.S. Real Estate Mortgage Investment Conduit (REMIC) Income Tax Return
- **Instructions for Forms 1120 and 1120-A**
- **Form 2553,** Election by a Small Business Corporation
- **Form 2848,** Power of Attorney and Declaration of Representative
- **Form 8821,** Tax Information Authorization
- **Form 8832,** Entity Classification Election
  For more **information** about filing Form SS-4 and related issues, see:
- **Circular A,** Agricultural Employer's Tax Guide (Pub. 51)
- **Circular E,** Employer's Tax Guide (Pub. 15)
- **Pub. 538,** Accounting Periods and Methods
- **Pub. 542,** Corporations
- **Pub. 557,** Exempt Status for Your Organization
- **Pub. 583,** Starting a Business and Keeping Records
- **Pub. 966,** Electronic Choices for Paying ALL Your Federal Taxes
- **Pub. 1635,** Understanding Your EIN
- **Package 1023,** Application for Recognition of Exemption Under Section 501(c)(3) of the Internal Revenue Code
- **Package 1024,** Application for Recognition of Exemption Under Section 501(a)

Specific Instructions

Print or type all entries on Form SS-4. Follow the instructions for each line to expedite processing and to avoid unnecessary IRS requests for additional information. Enter "N/A" (nonapplicable) on the lines that do not apply.

Line 1—Legal name of entity (or individual) for whom the EIN is being requested. Enter the legal name of the entity (or individual) applying for the EIN exactly as it appears on the social security card, charter, or other applicable legal document.

Individuals. Enter your first name, middle initial, and last name. If you are a sole proprietor, enter your individual name, not your business name. Enter your business name on line 2. Do not use abbreviations or nicknames on line 1.

Trusts. Enter the name of the trust.

Estate of a decedent. Enter the name of the estate.

Partnerships. Enter the legal name of the partnership as it appears in the partnership agreement.

Corporations. Enter the corporate name as it appears in the corporation charter or other legal document creating it.

Plan administrators. Enter the name of the plan administrator. A plan administrator who already has an EIN should use that number.

Line 2—Trade name of business. Enter the trade name of the business if different from the legal name. The trade name is the "doing business as " (DBA) name.

 *Use the full legal name shown on line 1 on all tax returns filed for the entity. (However, if you enter a trade name on line 2 and choose to use the trade name instead of the legal name, enter the trade name on **all returns** you file.) To prevent processing delays and errors, **always** use the legal name only (or the trade name only) on **all** tax returns.*

Line 3—Executor, trustee, "care of" name. Trusts enter the name of the trustee. Estates enter the name of the executor, administrator, or other fiduciary. If the entity applying has a designated person to receive tax information, enter that person's name as the "care of" person. Enter the individual's first name, middle initial, and last name.

Lines 4a-b—Mailing address. Enter the mailing address for the entity's correspondence. If line 3 is completed, enter the address for the executor, trustee or "care of" person. Generally, this address will be used on all tax returns.

 *File **Form 8822**, Change of Address, to report any subsequent changes to the entity's mailing address.*

Lines 5a-b—Street address. Provide the entity's physical address **only** if different from its mailing address shown in lines 4a-b. **Do not** enter a P.O. box number here.

Line 6—County and state where principal business is located. Enter the entity's primary **physical** location.

Lines 7a-b—Name of principal officer, general partner, grantor, owner, or trustor. Enter the first name, middle initial, last name, and SSN of **(a)** the principal officer if the business is a corporation, **(b)** a general partner if a partnership, **(c)** the owner of an entity that is disregarded as separate from its owner (disregarded entities owned by a corporation enter the corporation's name and EIN), or **(d)** a grantor, owner, or trustor if a trust.

If the person in question is an **alien individual** with a previously assigned individual taxpayer identification number (ITIN), enter the ITIN in the space provided and submit a copy of an official identifying document. If

necessary, complete **Form W-7,** Application for IRS Individual Taxpayer Identification Number, to obtain an ITIN.

You are **required** to enter an SSN, ITIN, or EIN unless the only reason you are applying for an EIN is to make an entity classification election (see Regulations sections 301.7701-1 through 301.7701-3) and you are a nonresident alien with no effectively connected income from sources within the United States.

Line 8a—Type of entity. Check the box that best describes the type of entity applying for the EIN. If you are an alien individual with an ITIN previously assigned to you, enter the ITIN in place of a requested SSN.

 *This is not an election for a tax classification of an entity. See **Limited liability company (LLC)** on page 4.*

Other. If not specifically listed, check the "Other" box, enter the type of entity and the type of return, if any, that will be filed (for example, "Common Trust Fund, Form 1065" or "Created a Pension Plan"). Do not enter "N/A." If you are an alien individual applying for an EIN, see the **Lines 7a-b** instructions above.
- **Household employer.** If you are an individual, check the "Other" box and enter "Household Employer" and your SSN. If you are a state or local agency serving as a tax reporting agent for public assistance recipients who become household employers, check the "Other" box and enter "Household Employer Agent." If you are a trust that qualifies as a household employer, you do not need a separate EIN for reporting tax information relating to household employees; use the EIN of the trust.
- **QSub.** For a qualified subchapter S subsidiary (QSub) check the "Other" box and specify "QSub."
- **Withholding agent.** If you are a withholding agent required to file Form 1042, check the "Other" box and enter "Withholding Agent."

Sole proprietor. Check this box if you file Schedule C, C-EZ, or F (Form 1040) and have a qualified plan, or are required to file excise, employment, alcohol, tobacco, or firearms returns, or are a payer of gambling winnings. Enter your SSN (or ITIN) in the space provided. If you are a nonresident alien with no effectively connected income from sources within the United States, you do not need to enter an SSN or ITIN.

Corporation. This box is for any corporation **other than a personal service corporation.** If you check this box, enter the income tax form number to be filed by the entity in the space provided.

 *If you entered "1120S" after the "Corporation" checkbox, the corporation **must** file Form 2553 **no later than the 15th day of the 3rd month of the tax year the election is to take effect.** Until Form 2553 has been received and approved, you will be considered a Form 1120 filer. See the Instructions for Form 2553.*

Personal service corp. Check this box if the entity is a personal service corporation. An entity is a personal service corporation for a tax year only if:

- The principal activity of the entity during the testing period (prior tax year) for the tax year is the performance of personal services substantially by employee-owners, and
- The employee-owners own at least 10% of the fair market value of the outstanding stock in the entity on the last day of the testing period.

Personal services include performance of services in such fields as health, law, accounting, or consulting. For more information about personal service corporations, see the Instructions for Forms 1120 and 1120-A and Pub. 542.

Other nonprofit organization. Check this box if the nonprofit organization is other than a church or church-controlled organization and specify the type of nonprofit organization (for example, an educational organization).

 *If the organization also seeks tax-exempt status, you **must** file either Package 1023 or Package 1024. See Pub. 557 for more information.*

If the organization is covered by a group exemption letter, enter the four-digit **group exemption number (GEN).** (Do not confuse the GEN with the nine-digit EIN.) If you do not know the GEN, contact the parent organization. Get Pub. 557 for more information about group exemption numbers.

Plan administrator. If the plan administrator is an individual, enter the plan administrator's SSN in the space provided.

REMIC. Check this box if the entity has elected to be treated as a real estate mortgage investment conduit (REMIC). See the Instructions for Form 1066 for more information.

Limited liability company (LLC). An LLC is an entity organized under the laws of a state or foreign country as a limited liability company. For Federal tax purposes, an LLC may be treated as a partnership or corporation or be disregarded as an entity separate from its owner.

By **default,** a domestic LLC with only one member is **disregarded** as an entity separate from its owner and must include all of its income and expenses on the owner's tax return (e.g., **Schedule C (Form 1040)**). Also by default, a domestic LLC with two or more members is treated as a partnership. A domestic LLC may file Form 8832 to avoid either default classification and elect to be classified as an association taxable as a corporation. For more information on entity classifications (including the rules for foreign entities), see the instructions for Form 8832.

 *Do not file Form 8832 if the LLC accepts the default classifications above. **However, if the LLC will be electing S Corporation status, it must timely file both Form 8832 and Form 2553.***

Complete Form SS-4 for LLCs as follows:
- A single-member domestic LLC that accepts the default classification (above) does not need an EIN and generally should not file Form SS-4. Generally, the LLC

should use the name and EIN of its **owner** for all Federal tax purposes. However, the reporting and payment of employment taxes for employees of the LLC may be made using the name and EIN of **either** the owner or the LLC as explained in Notice 99-6. You can find Notice 99-6 on page 12 of Internal Revenue Bulletin 1999-3 at **www.irs.gov/pub/irs-irbs/irb99-03.pdf. (Note:** If the LLC applicant indicates in box 13 that it has employees or expects to have employees, the owner (whether an individual or other entity) of a single-member domestic LLC will also be assigned its own EIN (if it does not already have one) even if the LLC will be filing the employment tax returns.)
- A single-member, domestic LLC that accepts the default classification (above) and wants an EIN for filing employment tax returns (see above) or non-Federal purposes, such as a state requirement, must check the "Other" box and write "Disregarded Entity" or, when applicable, "Disregarded Entity—Sole Proprietorship" in the space provided.
- A multi-member, domestic LLC that accepts the default classification (above) must check the "Partnership" box.
- A domestic LLC that will be filing Form 8832 to elect corporate status must check the "Corporation" box and write in "Single-Member" or "Multi-Member" immediately below the "form number" entry line.

Line 9—Reason for applying. Check only **one** box. Do not enter "N/A."

Started new business. Check this box if you are starting a new business that requires an EIN. If you check this box, enter the type of business being started. **Do not** apply if you already have an EIN and are only adding another place of business.

Hired employees. Check this box if the existing business is requesting an EIN because it has hired or is hiring employees and is therefore required to file employment tax returns. **Do not** apply if you already have an EIN and are only hiring employees. For information on employment taxes (e.g., for family members), see Circular E.

 You may be required to make electronic deposits of all depository taxes (such as employment tax, excise tax, and corporate income tax) using the Electronic Federal Tax Payment System (EFTPS). See section 11, Depositing Taxes, of Circular E and Pub. 966.

Created a pension plan. Check this box if you have created a pension plan and need an EIN for reporting purposes. Also, enter the type of plan in the space provided.

 Check this box if you are applying for a trust EIN when a new pension plan is established. In addition, check the "Other" box in line 8a and write "Created a Pension Plan" in the space provided.

Banking purpose. Check this box if you are requesting an EIN for banking purposes only, and enter the banking purpose (for example, a bowling league for depositing dues or an investment club for dividend and interest reporting).

Changed type of organization. Check this box if the business is changing its type of organization. For example, the business was a sole proprietorship and has been incorporated or has become a partnership. If you check this box, specify in the space provided (including available space immediately below) the type of change made. For example, "From Sole Proprietorship to Partnership."

Purchased going business. Check this box if you purchased an existing business. **Do not** use the former owner's EIN unless you became the "owner" of a corporation by acquiring its stock.

Created a trust. Check this box if you created a trust, and enter the type of trust created. For example, indicate if the trust is a nonexempt charitable trust or a split-interest trust.

Exception. Do **not** file this form for certain grantor-type trusts. The trustee does not need an EIN for the trust if the trustee furnishes the name and TIN of the grantor/owner and the address of the trust to all payors. See the Instructions for Form 1041 for more information.

 Do not check this box if you are applying for a trust EIN when a new pension plan is established. Check "Created a pension plan."

Other. Check this box if you are requesting an EIN for any other reason; and enter the reason. For example, a newly-formed state government entity should enter "Newly-Formed State Government Entity" in the space provided.

Line 10—Date business started or acquired. If you are starting a new business, enter the starting date of the business. If the business you acquired is already operating, enter the date you acquired the business. If you are changing the form of ownership of your business, enter the date the new ownership entity began. Trusts should enter the date the trust was legally created. Estates should enter the date of death of the decedent whose name appears on line 1 or the date when the estate was legally funded.

Line 11—Closing month of accounting year. Enter the last month of your accounting year or tax year. An accounting or tax year is usually 12 consecutive months, either a calendar year or a fiscal year (including a period of 52 or 53 weeks). A calendar year is 12 consecutive months ending on December 31. A fiscal year is either 12 consecutive months ending on the last day of any month other than December or a 52-53 week year. For more information on accounting periods, see Pub. 538.

Individuals. Your tax year generally will be a calendar year.

Partnerships. Partnerships must adopt one of the following tax years:
* The tax year of the majority of its partners,
* The tax year common to all of its principal partners,
* The tax year that results in the least aggregate deferral of income, or
* In certain cases, some other tax year.

See the Instructions for Form 1065 for more information.

REMICs. REMICs must have a calendar year as their tax year.

Personal service corporations. A personal service corporation generally must adopt a calendar year unless:
* It can establish a business purpose for having a different tax year, or
* It elects under section 444 to have a tax year other than a calendar year.

Trusts. Generally, a trust must adopt a calendar year except for the following:
* Tax-exempt trusts,
* Charitable trusts, and
* Grantor-owned trusts.

Line 12—First date wages or annuities were paid or will be paid. If the business has or will have employees, enter the date on which the business began or will begin to pay wages. If the business does not plan to have employees, enter "N/A."

Withholding agent. Enter the date you began or will begin to pay income (including annuities) to a nonresident alien. This also applies to individuals who are required to file Form 1042 to report alimony paid to a nonresident alien.

Line 13—Highest number of employees expected in the next 12 months. Complete each box by entering the number (including zero ("-0-")) of "Agricultural," "Household," or "Other" employees expected by the applicant in the next 12 months. For a definition of agricultural labor (farmwork), see Circular A.

Lines 14 and 15. Check the **one** box in line 14 that best describes the principal activity of the applicant's business. Check the "Other" box (and specify the applicant's principal activity) if none of the listed boxes applies.

Use line 15 to describe the applicant's principal line of business in more detail. For example, if you checked the "Construction" box in line 14, enter additional detail such as "General contractor for residential buildings" in line 15.

Construction. Check this box if the applicant is engaged in erecting buildings or other structures, (e.g., streets, highways, bridges, tunnels). The term "Construction" also includes special trade contractors, (e.g., plumbing, HVAC, electrical, carpentry, concrete, excavation, etc. contractors).

Real estate. Check this box if the applicant is engaged in renting or leasing real estate to others; managing, selling, buying or renting real estate for others; or providing related real estate services (e.g., appraisal services).

Rental and leasing. Check this box if the applicant is engaged in providing tangible goods such as autos, computers, consumer goods, or industrial machinery and equipment to customers in return for a periodic rental or lease payment.

Manufacturing. Check this box if the applicant is engaged in the mechanical, physical, or chemical transformation of materials, substances, or components into new products. The assembling of component parts of manufactured products is also considered to be manufacturing.

Transportation & warehousing. Check this box if the applicant provides transportation of passengers or cargo; warehousing or storage of goods; scenic or sight-seeing transportation; or support activities related to these modes of transportation.

Finance & insurance. Check this box if the applicant is engaged in transactions involving the creation, liquidation, or change of ownership of financial assets and/or facilitating such financial transactions; underwriting annuities/insurance policies; facilitating such underwriting by selling insurance policies; or by providing other insurance or employee-benefit related services.

Health care and social assistance. Check this box if the applicant is engaged in providing physical, medical, or psychiatric care using licensed health care professionals or providing social assistance activities such as youth centers, adoption agencies, individual/family services, temporary shelters, etc.

Accommodation & food services. Check this box if the applicant is engaged in providing customers with lodging, meal preparation, snacks, or beverages for immediate consumption.

Wholesale–agent/broker. Check this box if the applicant is engaged in arranging for the purchase or sale of goods owned by others or purchasing goods on a commission basis for goods traded in the wholesale market, usually between businesses.

Wholesale–other. Check this box if the applicant is engaged in selling goods in the wholesale market generally to other businesses for resale on their own account.

Retail. Check this box if the applicant is engaged in selling merchandise to the general public from a fixed store; by direct, mail-order, or electronic sales; or by using vending machines.

Other. Check this box if the applicant is engaged in an activity not described above. Describe the applicant's principal business activity in the space provided.

Lines 16a-c. Check the applicable box in line 16a to indicate whether or not the entity (or individual) applying for an EIN was issued one previously. Complete lines 16b and 16c **only** if the "Yes" box in line 16a is checked. If the applicant previously applied for **more than one** EIN, write "See Attached" in the empty space in line 16a and attach a separate sheet providing the line 16b and 16c information for each EIN previously requested.

Third Party Designee. Complete this section **only** if you want to authorize the named individual to receive the entity's EIN and answer questions about the completion of Form SS-4. The designee's authority terminates at the time the EIN is assigned and released to the designee. **You must complete the signature area for the authorization to be valid.**

Signature. When required, the application must be signed by **(a)** the individual, if the applicant is an individual, **(b)** the president, vice president, or other principal officer, if the applicant is a corporation, **(c)** a responsible and duly authorized member or officer having knowledge of its affairs, if the applicant is a partnership, government entity, or other unincorporated organization, or **(d)** the fiduciary, if the applicant is a trust or an estate. Foreign applicants may have any duly-authorized person, (e.g., division manager), sign Form SS-4.

Privacy Act and Paperwork Reduction Act Notice. We ask for the information on this form to carry out the Internal Revenue laws of the United States. We need it to comply with section 6109 and the regulations thereunder which generally require the inclusion of an employer identification number (EIN) on certain returns, statements, or other documents filed with the Internal Revenue Service. If your entity is required to obtain an EIN, you are required to provide all of the information requested on this form. Information on this form may be used to determine which Federal tax returns you are required to file and to provide you with related forms and publications.

We disclose this form to the Social Security Administration for their use in determining compliance with applicable laws. We may give this information to the Department of Justice for use in civil and criminal litigation, and to the cities, states, and the District of Columbia for use in administering their tax laws. We may also disclose this information to Federal and state agencies to enforce Federal nontax criminal laws and to combat terrorism.

We will be unable to issue an EIN to you unless you provide all of the requested information which applies to your entity. Providing false information could subject you to penalties.

You are not required to provide the information requested on a form that is subject to the Paperwork Reduction Act unless the form displays a valid OMB control number. Books or records relating to a form or its instructions must be retained as long as their contents may become material in the administration of any Internal Revenue law. Generally, tax returns and return information are confidential, as required by section 6103.

The time needed to complete and file this form will vary depending on individual circumstances. The estimated average time is:

Recordkeeping	6 min.
Learning about the law or the form	22 min.
Preparing the form	46 min.
Copying, assembling, and sending the form to the IRS	20 min.

If you have comments concerning the accuracy of these time estimates or suggestions for making this form simpler, we would be happy to hear from you. You can write to the Tax Products Coordinating Committee, Western Area Distribution Center, Rancho Cordova, CA 95743-0001. **Do not** send the form to this address. Instead, see **How To Apply** on page 1.

WAIVER OF NOTICE
OF THE ORGANIZATIONAL MEETING
OF

_____

We, the undersigned incorporators named in the certificate of incorporation of the above-named corporation, hereby agree and consent that the organization meeting of the corporation be held on the date and time and place stated below, and hereby waive all notice of such meeting and of any adjournment thereof.

Place of meeting: _____

Date of Meeting: _____

Time of meeting: _____

Dated: _____

_____
Incorporator

_____
Incorporator

_____
Incorporator

This page intentionally blank.

MINUTES OF THE ORGANIZATIONAL MEETING OF
INCORPORATORS AND DIRECTORS OF

_____

The organization meeting of the above corporation was held on _____,
20_____ at _____ at _____ o'clock __m.

The following persons were present:

_____   _____
_____   _____
_____   _____

The Waiver of notice of this meeting was signed by all directors and incorporators named in the Articles of Incorporation and filed in the minute book.

The meeting was called to order by _____, an Incorporator named in the Articles of Incorporation. _____ was nominated and elected Chairman, and acted as such until relieved by the president. _____ was nominated and elected temporary secretary, and acted as such until relieved by the permanent secretary.

A copy of the Articles of Incorporation, which was filed with the Secretary of State of the State of _____ on _____, 20_____, was examined by the Directors and Incorporators and filed in the minute book.

The election of officers for the coming year was then held and the following were duly nominated and elected by the Board of Directors to be the officers of the corporation, to serve until such time as their successors are elected and qualified:

President: _____
Vice President: _____
Secretary: _____
Treasurer: _____

The proposed Bylaws for the corporation were then presented to the meeting and discussed. Upon motion duly made, seconded and carried, the Bylaws were adopted and added to the minute book.

A corporate seal for the corporation was then presented to the meeting and upon motion duly made, seconded and carried, it was adopted as the seal of the corporation. An impression thereof was then made in the margin of these minutes.

(Seal)

The necessity of opening a bank account was then discussed and upon motion duly made, seconded, and carried, the following resolution was adopted:

RESOLVED that the corporation open bank accounts with _____ _____ and that the officers of the corporation are authorized to take such action as is necessary to open such accounts; that the bank's printed form of resolution is hereby adopted and incorporated into these minutes by reference and shall be placed in the minute book; that any _____ of the following persons shall have signature authority over the account:

_____   _____

_____   _____

_____   _____

_____   _____

Proposed stock certificates and stock transfer ledger were then presented to the meeting and examined. Upon motion duly made, seconded, and carried the stock certificates and ledger were adopted as the certificates and transfer book to be used by the corporation. A sample stock certificate marked "VOID" and the stock transfer ledger were then added to the minute book. Upon motion duly made, seconded, and carried, it was then resolved that the stock certificates, when issued, would be signed by the President and the Secretary of the corporation.

The tax status of the corporation was then discussed and it was moved, seconded, and carried that the stock of the corporation be issued under §1244 of the Internal Revenue Code and that the officers of the corporation take the necessary action to:

1.   Obtain an employer tax number by filing form SS-4

2.   ❏ Become an S corporation for tax purposes
      ❏ Remain a C corporation for tax purposes

The expenses of organizing the corporation were then discussed and it was moved, seconded, and carried that the corporation pay in full from the corporate funds the expenses and reimburse any advances made by the incorporators upon proof of payment.

The Directors named in the Articles of Incorporation then tendered their resignations, effective upon the adjournment of this meeting. Upon motion duly made, seconded and carried, the following named persons were elected as Directors of the corporation, each to hold office until the first annual meeting of shareholders, and until a successor of each shall have been elected and qualified.

_____

_____

_____

There were presented to the corporation, the following offer(s) to purchase shares of capital stock:

FROM	NUMBER OF SHARES	CONSIDERATION
_____	_____	_____
_____	_____	_____
_____	_____	_____
_____	_____	_____

The offers were discussed and after motion duly made, seconded, and carried were approved. It was further resolved that the Board of Directors has determined that the consideration was valued at least equal to the value of the shares to be issued and that upon tender of the consideration, fully paid nonassessable shares of the corporation be issued.

There being no further business before the meeting, on motion duly made, seconded and carried, the meeting adjourned.

DATED: _____

_____
President

_____
Secretary

This page intentionally blank.

BYLAWS OF

_____

A _____ CORPORATION

ARTICLE I—OFFICES

The principal office of the Corporation shall be located in the City of _____ _____ and the State of _____. The Corporation may also maintain offices at such other places as the Board of Directors may, from time to time, determine.

ARTICLE II—SHAREHOLDERS

Section 1—Annual Meetings: The annual meeting of the shareholders of the Corporation shall be held each year on _____ at _____ m. at the principal office of the Corporation or at such other places, within or without the State of _____, as the Board may authorize, for the purpose of electing directors, and transacting such other business as may properly come before the meeting.

Section 2—Special Meetings: Special meetings of the shareholders may be called at any time by the Board, the President, or by the holders of twenty-five percent (25%) of the shares then outstanding and entitled to vote.

Section 3—Place of Meetings: All meetings of shareholders shall be held at the principal office of the Corporation, or at such other places as the board shall designate in the notice of such meetings.

Section 4—Notice of Meetings: Written or printed notice stating the place, day, and hour of the meeting and, in the case of a special meeting, the purpose of the meeting, shall be delivered personally or by mail not less than ten days, nor more than sixty days, before the date of the meeting. Notice shall be given to each Member of record entitled to vote at the meeting. If mailed, such notice shall be deemed to have been delivered when deposited in the United States Mail with postage paid and addressed to the Member at his or her address as it appears on the records of the Corporation.

Section 5—Waiver of Notice: A written waiver of notice signed by a Member, whether before or after a meeting, shall be equivalent to the giving of such notice. Attendance of a Member at a meeting shall constitute a waiver of notice of such meeting, except when the Member attends for the express purpose of objecting, at the beginning of the meeting, to the transaction of any business because the meeting is not lawfully called or convened.

Section 6—Quorum: Except as otherwise provided by Statute, or the Articles of Incorporation, at all meetings of shareholders of the Corporation, the presence at the commencement of such meetings in person or by proxy of shareholders of record holding a majority of the total number of shares of the Corporation then issued and outstanding and entitled to vote, but in no event less than one-third of the shares entitled to vote at the meeting, shall constitute a quorum for the transaction of any business. If any shareholder leaves after the commencement of a meeting, this shall have no effect on the existence of a quorum, after a quorum has been established at such meeting.

Despite the absence of a quorum at any annual or special meeting of shareholders, the shareholders, by a majority of the votes cast by the holders of shares entitled to vote thereon, may adjourn the meeting. At any such adjourned meeting at which a quorum is present, any business may be transacted at the meeting as originally called as if a quorum had been present.

Section 7—Voting: Except as otherwise provided by Statute or by the Articles of Incorporation, any corporate action, other than the election of directors, to be taken by vote of the shareholders, shall be authorized by a majority of votes cast at a meeting of shareholders by the holders of shares entitled to vote thereon.

Except as otherwise provided by Statute or by the Articles of Incorporation, at each meeting of shareholders, each holder of record of stock of the Corporation entitled to vote thereat, shall be entitled to one vote for each share of stock registered in his or her name on the stock transfer books of the corporation.

Each shareholder entitled to vote may do so by proxy; provided, however, that the instrument authorizing such proxy to act shall have been executed in writing by the shareholder him- or herself. No proxy shall be valid after the expiration of eleven months from the date of its execution, unless the person executing it shall have specified therein, the length of time it is to continue in force. Such instrument shall be exhibited to the Secretary at the meeting and shall be filed with the records of the corporation.

Any resolution in writing, signed by all of the shareholders entitled to vote thereon, shall be and constitute action by such shareholders to the effect therein expressed, with the same force and effect as if the same had been duly passed by unanimous vote at a duly called meeting of shareholders and such resolution so signed shall be inserted in the Minute Book of the Corporation under its proper date.

ARTICLE III—BOARD OF DIRECTORS

Section 1—Number, Election and Term of Office: The number of the directors of the Corporation shall be (____). This number may be increased or decreased by the amendment of these bylaws by the Board but shall in no case be less than _____ director(s). The members of the Board, who need not be shareholders, shall be elected by a majority of the votes cast at a meeting of shareholders entitled to vote in the election. Each director shall hold office until the annual meeting of the shareholders next succeeding his election, and until his successor is elected and qualified, or until his prior death, resignation or removal.

Section 2—Vacancies: Any vacancy in the Board shall be filled for the unexpired portion of the term by a majority vote of the remaining directors, though less than a quorum, at any regular meeting or special meeting of the Board called for that purpose. Any such director so elected may be replaced by the shareholders at a regular or special meeting of shareholders.

Section 3—Duties and Powers: The Board shall be responsible for the control and management of the affairs, property and interests of the Corporation, and may exercise all powers of the Corporation, except as limited by statute.

Section 4—Annual Meetings: An annual meeting of the Board shall be held immediately following the annual meeting of the shareholders, at the place of such annual meeting of shareholders. The Board from time to time, may provide by resolution for the holding of other meetings of the Board, and may fix the time and place thereof.

Section 5—Special Meetings: Special meetings of the Board shall be held whenever called by the President or by one of the directors, at such time and place as may be specified in the respective notice or waivers of notice thereof.

Section 6—Notice and Waiver: Notice of any special meeting shall be given at least five days prior thereto by written notice delivered personally, by mail, or by telegram to each Director at his or her address. If mailed, such notice shall be deemed to be delivered when deposited in the United States Mail with postage prepaid. If notice is given by telegram, such notice shall be deemed to be delivered when the telegram is delivered to the telegraph company.

Any Director may waive notice of any meeting, either before, at, or after such meeting, by signing a waiver of notice. The attendance of a Director at a meeting shall constitute a waiver of notice of such meeting and a waiver of any and all objections to the place of such meeting, or the manner in which it has been called or convened, except when a Director states at the beginning of the meeting any objection to the transaction of business because the meeting is not lawfully called or convened.

Section 7—Chairman: The Board may, at its discretion, elect a Chairman. At all meetings of the Board, the Chairman of the Board, if any and if present, shall preside. If there is no Chairman, or he or she is absent, then the President shall preside, and in his or her absence, a Chairman chosen by the directors shall preside.

Section 8—Quorum and Adjournments: At all meetings of the Board, the presence of a majority of the entire Board shall be necessary and sufficient to constitute a quorum for the transaction of business, except as otherwise provided by law, by the Articles of Incorporation, or by these bylaws. A majority of the directors present at the time and place of any regular or special meeting, although less than a quorum, may adjourn the same from time to time without notice, until a quorum shall be present.

Section 9—Board Action: At all meetings of the Board, each director present shall have one vote, irrespective of the number of shares of stock, if any, which he may hold. Except as otherwise provided by Statute, the action of a majority of the directors present at any meeting at which a quorum is present shall be the act of the Board. Any action authorized, in writing, by all of the Directors entitled to vote thereon and filed with the minutes of the Corporation shall be the act of the Board with the same force and effect as if the same had been passed by unanimous vote at a duly called meeting of the Board. Any action taken by the Board may be taken without a meeting if agreed to in writing by all members before or after the action is taken and if a record of such action is filed in the minute book.

Section 10—Telephone Meetings: Directors may participate in meetings of the Board through use of a telephone if such can be arranged so that all Board members can hear all other members. The use of a telephone for participation shall constitute presence in person.

Section 11—Resignation and Removal: Any director may resign at any time by giving written notice to another Board member, the President or the Secretary of the Corporation. Unless otherwise specified in such written notice, such resignation shall take effect upon receipt thereof by the Board or by such officer, and the acceptance of such resignation shall not be necessary to make it effective. Any director may be removed with or without cause at any time by the affirmative vote of shareholders holding of record in the aggregate at least a majority of the outstanding shares of the Corporation at a special meeting of the shareholders called for that purpose, and may be removed for cause by action of the Board.

Section 12—Compensation: No stated salary shall be paid to directors, as such for their services, but by resolution of the Board a fixed sum and/or expenses of attendance, if any, may be allowed for attendance at each regular or special meeting of the Board. Nothing herein contained shall be construed to preclude any director from serving the Corporation in any other capacity and receiving compensation therefor.

ARTICLE IV—OFFICERS

Section 1—Number, Qualification, Election and Term: The officers of the Corporation shall consist of a President, a Secretary, a Treasurer, and such other officers, as the Board may from time to time deem advisable. Any officer may be, but is not required to be, a director of the Corporation. The officers of the Corporation shall be elected by the Board at the regular annual meeting of the Board. Each officer shall hold office until the annual meeting of the Board next succeeding his or her election, and until his or her successor shall have been elected and qualified, or until his or her death, resignation, or removal.

Section 2—Resignation and Removal: Any officer may resign at any time by giving written notice of such resignation to the President or the Secretary of the Corporation or to a member of the Board. Unless otherwise specified in such written notice, such resignation shall take effect upon receipt thereof by the Board member or by such officer, and the acceptance of such resignation shall not be necessary to make it effective. Any officer may be removed, either with or without cause, and a successor elected by a majority vote of the Board at any time.

Section 3—Vacancies: A vacancy in any office may at any time be filled for the unexpired portion of the term by a majority vote of the Board.

Section 4—Duties of Officers: Officers of the Corporation shall, unless otherwise provided by the Board, each have such powers and duties as generally pertain to their respective offices as well as such powers and duties as may from time to time be specifically decided by the Board. The President shall be the chief executive officer of the Corporation.

Section 5—Compensation: The officers of the Corporation shall be entitled to such compensation as the Board shall from time to time determine.

Section 6—Delegation of Duties: In the absence or disability of any Officer of the Corporation or for any other reason deemed sufficient by the Board of Directors, the Board may delegate his or her powers or duties to any other Officer or to any other Director.

Section 7—Shares of Other Corporations: Whenever the Corporation is the holder of shares of any other Corporation, any right or power of the Corporation as such shareholder (including the attendance, acting and voting at shareholders' meetings and execution of waivers, consents, proxies or other instruments) may be exercised on behalf of the Corporation by the President, any Vice President, or such other person as the Board may authorize.

ARTICLE V—COMMITTEES

The Board of Directors may, by resolution, designate an Executive Committee and one or more other committees. Such committees shall have such functions and may exercise such power of the Board of Directors as can be lawfully delegated, and to the extent provided in the resolution or resolutions creating such committee or committees. Meetings of committees may be held without notice at such time and at such place as shall from time to time be determined by the committees. The committees of the corporation shall keep regular minutes of their proceedings, and report these minutes to the Board of Directors when required.

ARTICLE VI—BOOKS, RECORDS, AND REPORTS

Section 1—Annual Report: The Corporation shall send an annual report to the Members of the Corporation not later than _____ months after the close of each fiscal year of the Corporation. Such report shall include a balance sheet as of the close of the fiscal year of the Corporation and a revenue and disbursement statement for the year ending on such closing date. Such financial statements shall be prepared from and in accordance with the books of the Corporation, and in conformity with generally accepted accounting principles applied on a consistent basis.

Section 2—Permanent Records: The corporation shall keep current and correct records of the accounts, minutes of the meetings and proceedings and membership records of the corporation. Such records shall be kept at the registered office or the principal place of business of the corporation. Any such records shall be in written form or in a form capable of being converted into written form.

Section 3—Inspection of Corporate Records: Any person who is a Voting Member of the Corporation shall have the right at any reasonable time, and on written demand stating the purpose thereof, to examine and make copies from the relevant books and records of accounts, minutes, and records of the Corporation. Upon the written request of any Voting Member, the Corporation shall mail to such Member a copy of the most recent balance sheet and revenue and disbursement statement.

ARTICLE VII—SHARES OF STOCK

Section 1—Certificates: Each shareholder of the corporation shall be entitled to have a certificate representing all shares which he or she owns. The form of such certificate shall be adopted by a majority vote of the Board of Directors and shall be signed by the President and Secretary of the Corporation and sealed with the seal of the corporation. No certificate representing shares shall be issued until the full amount of consideration therefore has been paid.

Section 2—Stock Ledger: The corporation shall maintain a ledger of the stock records of the Corporation. Transfers of shares of the Corporation shall be made on the stock ledger of the Corporation only at the direction of the holder of record upon surrender of the outstanding certificate(s). The Corporation shall be entitled to treat the holder of record of any share or shares as the absolute owner thereof for all purposes and, accordingly, shall not be bound to recognize any legal, equitable or other claim to, or interest in, such share or shares on the part of any other person, whether or not it shall have express or other notice thereof, except as otherwise expressly provided by law.

ARTICLE VIII—DIVIDENDS

Upon approval by the Board of Directors the corporation may pay dividends on its shares in the form of cash, property or additional shares at any time that the corporation is solvent and if such dividends would not render the corporation insolvent.

ARTICLE IX—FISCAL YEAR

The fiscal year of the Corporation shall be the period selected by the Board of Directors as the tax year of the Corporation for federal income tax purposes.

ARTICLE X—CORPORATE SEAL

The Board of Directors may adopt, use and modify a corporate seal. Failure to affix the seal to corporate documents shall not affect the validity of such document.

ARTICLE XI—AMENDMENTS

The Articles of Incorporation may be amended by the Shareholders as provided by _____ statutes. These Bylaws may be altered, amended, or replaced by the Board of Directors; provided, however, that any Bylaws or amendments thereto as adopted by the Board of Directors may be altered, amended, or repealed by vote of the Shareholders. Bylaws adopted by the Members may not be amended or repealed by the Board.

ARTICLE XII—INDEMNIFICATION

Any officer, director or employee of the Corporation shall be indemnified to the full extent allowed by the laws of the State of _____.

Certified to be the Bylaws of the corporation adopted by the Board of Directors on _____, 20____.

_____
Secretary

This page intentionally blank.

Banking Resolution of

_____

The undersigned, being the Corporate Secretary of the above corporation, hereby certifies that on the _____ day of _____, 20_____, the Board of Directors of the corporation adopted the following resolution:

RESOLVED that the corporation open bank accounts with _____ _____ and that the officers of the corporation are authorized to take such action as is necessary to open such accounts; that the bank's printed form of resolution is hereby adopted and incorporated into these minutes by reference and shall be placed in the minute book; that any _____ of the following persons shall have signature authority over the account:

_____   _____

_____   _____

and that said resolution has not been modified or rescinded.

Date: _____

_____
Corporate Secretary

[Seal]

This page intentionally blank.

Offer to Purchase Stock

Date: _____

To the Board of Directors of

_____

The undersigned, hereby offers to purchase _____ shares of the
_____ stock of your corporation at a total purchase price of
_____.

Very truly yours,

_____

- -

Offer to Sell Stock
Pursuant to Sec. 1244 I.R.C.

Date: _____

To: _____

Dear _____,

The corporation hereby offers to sell to you _____ shares of its common
stock at a price of $_____ per share. These shares are issued pursuant to
Section 1244 of the Internal Revenue Code.

Your signature below shall constitute an acceptance of our offer as of the date it is
received by the corporation.

Very truly yours,

_____

By: _____

Accepted:

_____

This page intentionally blank.

Resolution
of

_____

a _____ **Corporation**

RESOLVED that the corporation shall reimburse the following parties for the organizational expenses of the organizers of this corporation and that the corporation shall amortize these expenses as allowed by IRS regulations.

Name   Expense   Amount

_____   _____ $_____

_____   _____ $_____

_____   _____ $_____

_____   _____ $_____

_____   _____ $_____

Date: _____

_____

_____

_____

_____

_____

This page intentionally blank.

Bill of Sale

The undersigned, in consideration of the issuance of _____ shares of common stock of _____, a _____ corporation, hereby grants, bargains, sells, transfers, and delivers unto said corporation the following goods and chattels:

To have and to hold the same forever.

And the undersigned, their heirs, successors, and administrators, covenant and warrant that they are the lawful owners of the said goods and chattels, and that they are free from all encumbrances. That the undersigned have the right to sell this property and that they will warrant and defend the sale of said property against the lawful claims and demands of all persons.

IN WITNESS whereof the undersigned have executed this Bill of Sale this _____ day of _____, 20_____.

_____

_____

_____

This page intentionally blank.

Form **2553**
(Rev. March 2005)

Department of the Treasury
Internal Revenue Service

Election by a Small Business Corporation

(Under section 1362 of the Internal Revenue Code)

▶ See Parts II and III on back and the separate instructions.

▶ The corporation may either send or fax this form to the IRS. See page 2 of the instructions.

OMB No. 1545-0146

Notes:
1. **Do not** file **Form 1120S,** U.S. Income Tax Return for an S Corporation, for any tax year before the year the election takes effect.
2. This election to be an S corporation can be accepted only if all the tests are met under **Who May Elect** on page 1 of the instructions; all shareholders have signed the consent statement; an officer has signed this form; and the exact name and address of the corporation and other required form information are provided.

Part I   Election Information

Please Type or Print

Name (see instructions)	**A** Employer identification number
Number, street, and room or suite no. (If a P.O. box, see instructions.)	**B** Date incorporated
City or town, state, and ZIP code	**C** State of incorporation

D Check the applicable box(es) if the corporation, after applying for the EIN shown in **A** above, changed its name ☐ or address ☐

E Election is to be effective for tax year beginning (month, day, year) . . . . ▶   /   /

F Name and title of officer or legal representative who the IRS may call for more information

G Telephone number of officer or legal representative

(   )

H If this election takes effect for the first tax year the corporation exists, enter month, day, and year of the **earliest** of the following: (1) date the corporation first had shareholders, (2) date the corporation first had assets, or (3) date the corporation began doing business . . . . ▶   /   /

I Selected tax year: Annual return will be filed for tax year ending (month and day) ▶..

If the tax year ends on any date other than December 31, except for a 52-53-week tax year ending with reference to the month of December, complete Part II on the back. If the date you enter is the ending date of a 52-53-week tax year, write "52-53-week year" to the right of the date.

J Name and address of each shareholder or former shareholder required to consent to the election. (See the instructions for column K)	**K** Shareholders' Consent Statement. Under penalties of perjury, we declare that we consent to the election of the above-named corporation to be an S corporation under section 1362(a) and that we have examined this consent statement, including accompanying schedules and statements, and to the best of our knowledge and belief, it is true, correct, and complete. We understand our consent is binding and may not be withdrawn after the corporation has made a valid election. (Sign and date below.)		**L** Stock owned or percentage of ownership (see instructions)		**M** Social security number or employer identification number (see instructions)	**N** Share-holder's tax year ends (month and day)
	Signature	Date	Number of shares or percentage of ownership	Date(s) acquired		

Under penalties of perjury, I declare that I have examined this election, including accompanying schedules and statements, and to the best of my knowledge and belief, it is true, correct, and complete.

Signature of officer ▶   Title ▶   Date ▶

For Paperwork Reduction Act Notice, see page 4 of the instructions.   Cat. No. 18629R   Form **2553** (Rev. 3-2005)

Part II — Selection of Fiscal Tax Year (All corporations using this part must complete item O and item P, Q, or R.)

O Check the applicable box to indicate whether the corporation is:

1. ☐ A new corporation **adopting** the tax year entered in item I, Part I.

2. ☐ An existing corporation **retaining** the tax year entered in item I, Part I.

3. ☐ An existing corporation **changing** to the tax year entered in item I, Part I.

P Complete item P if the corporation is using the automatic approval provisions of Rev. Proc. 2002-38, 2002-22 I.R.B. 1037, to request **(1)** a natural business year (as defined in section 5.05 of Rev. Proc. 2002-38) or **(2)** a year that satisfies the ownership tax year test (as defined in section 5.06 of Rev. Proc. 2002-38). Check the applicable box below to indicate the representation statement the corporation is making.

1. Natural Business Year ▶ ☐ I represent that the corporation is adopting, retaining, or changing to a tax year that qualifies as its natural business year as defined in section 5.05 of Rev. Proc. 2002-38 and has attached a statement verifying that it satisfies the 25% gross receipts test (see instructions for content of statement). I also represent that the corporation is not precluded by section 4.02 of Rev. Proc. 2002-38 from obtaining automatic approval of such adoption, retention, or change in tax year.

2. Ownership Tax Year ▶ ☐ I represent that shareholders (as described in section 5.06 of Rev. Proc. 2002-38) holding more than half of the shares of the stock (as of the first day of the tax year to which the request relates) of the corporation have the same tax year or are concurrently changing to the tax year that the corporation adopts, retains, or changes to per item I, Part I, and that such tax year satisfies the requirement of section 4.01(3) of Rev. Proc. 2002-38. I also represent that the corporation is not precluded by section 4.02 of Rev. Proc. 2002-38 from obtaining automatic approval of such adoption, retention, or change in tax year.

Note: *If you do not use item P and the corporation wants a fiscal tax year, complete either item Q or R below. Item Q is used to request a fiscal tax year based on a business purpose and to make a back-up section 444 election. Item R is used to make a regular section 444 election.*

Q Business Purpose—To request a fiscal tax year based on a business purpose, check box Q1. See instructions for details including payment of a user fee. You may also check box Q2 and/or box Q3.

1. Check here ▶ ☐ if the fiscal year entered in item I, Part I, is requested under the prior approval provisions of Rev. Proc. 2002-39, 2002-22 I.R.B. 1046. Attach to Form 2553 a statement describing the relevant facts and circumstances and, if applicable, the gross receipts from sales and services necessary to establish a business purpose. See the instructions for details regarding the gross receipts from sales and services. If the IRS proposes to disapprove the requested fiscal year, do you want a conference with the IRS National Office?
☐ Yes ☐ No

2. Check here ▶ ☐ to show that the corporation intends to make a back-up section 444 election in the event the corporation's business purpose request is not approved by the IRS. (See instructions for more information.)

3. Check here ▶ ☐ to show that the corporation agrees to adopt or change to a tax year ending December 31 if necessary for the IRS to accept this election for S corporation status in the event (1) the corporation's business purpose request is not approved and the corporation makes a back-up section 444 election, but is ultimately not qualified to make a section 444 election, or (2) the corporation's business purpose request is not approved and the corporation did not make a back-up section 444 election.

R Section 444 Election—To make a section 444 election, check box R1. You may also check box R2.

1. Check here ▶ ☐ to show the corporation will make, if qualified, a section 444 election to have the fiscal tax year shown in item I, Part I. To make the election, you must complete **Form 8716,** Election To Have a Tax Year Other Than a Required Tax Year, and either attach it to Form 2553 or file it separately.

2. Check here ▶ ☐ to show that the corporation agrees to adopt or change to a tax year ending December 31 if necessary for the IRS to accept this election for S corporation status in the event the corporation is ultimately not qualified to make a section 444 election.

Part III — Qualified Subchapter S Trust (QSST) Election Under Section 1361(d)(2)*

Income beneficiary's name and address	Social security number
Trust's name and address	Employer identification number

Date on which stock of the corporation was transferred to the trust (month, day, year) . . . . ▶ / /

In order for the trust named above to be a QSST and thus a qualifying shareholder of the S corporation for which this Form 2553 is filed, I hereby make the election under section 1361(d)(2). Under penalties of perjury, I certify that the trust meets the definitional requirements of section 1361(d)(3) and that all other information provided in Part III is true, correct, and complete.

_____ _____
Signature of income beneficiary or signature and title of legal representative or other qualified person making the election   Date

*Use Part III to make the QSST election only if stock of the corporation has been transferred to the trust on or before the date on which the corporation makes its election to be an S corporation. The QSST election must be made and filed separately if stock of the corporation is transferred to the trust **after** the date on which the corporation makes the S election.

Instructions for Form 2553

(Rev. March 2005)

Election by a Small Business Corporation

**Department of the Treasury
Internal Revenue Service**

Section references are to the Internal Revenue Code unless otherwise noted.

General Instructions

Purpose

A corporation or other entity eligible to elect to be treated as a corporation must use Form 2553 to make an election under section 1362(a) to be an S corporation. An entity eligible to elect to be treated as a corporation that meets certain tests discussed below will be treated as a corporation as of the effective date of the S corporation election and does not need to file Form 8832, Entity Classification Election.

The income of an S corporation generally is taxed to the shareholders of the corporation rather than to the corporation itself. However, an S corporation may still owe tax on certain income. For details, see *Tax and Payments* in the Instructions for Form 1120S, U.S. Income Tax Return for an S Corporation.

Who May Elect

A corporation or other entity eligible to elect to be treated as a corporation may elect to be an S corporation only if it meets all the following tests.

1. It is (a) a domestic corporation, or (b) a domestic entity eligible to elect to be treated as a corporation that timely files Form 2553 and meets all the other tests listed below. If Form 2553 is not timely filed, see Rev. Proc. 2004-48, 2004-32 I.R.B. 172.

2. It has no more than 100 shareholders. A husband and wife (and their estates) are treated as one shareholder for this test. A member of a family can elect under section 1361(c)(1) to treat all members of the family as one shareholder for this test. All other persons are treated as separate shareholders.

3. Its only shareholders are individuals, estates, exempt organizations described in section 401(a) or 501(c)(3), or certain trusts described in section 1361(c)(2)(A).

For information about the section 1361(d)(2) election to be a qualified subchapter S trust (QSST), see the instructions for Part III. For information about the section 1361(e)(3) election to be an electing small business trust (ESBT), see Regulations section 1.1361-1(m). For guidance on how to convert a QSST to an ESBT, see Regulations section 1.1361-1(j)(12). If these elections were not timely made, see Rev. Proc. 2003-43, 2003-23 I.R.B. 998.

4. It has no nonresident alien shareholders.

5. It has only one class of stock (disregarding differences in voting rights). Generally, a corporation is treated as having only one class of stock if all outstanding shares of the corporation's stock confer identical rights to distribution and liquidation proceeds. See Regulations section 1.1361-1(l) for details.

6. It is not one of the following ineligible corporations.

a. A bank or thrift institution that uses the reserve method of accounting for bad debts under section 585.

b. An insurance company subject to tax under subchapter L of the Code.

c. A corporation that has elected to be treated as a possessions corporation under section 936.

d. A domestic international sales corporation (DISC) or former DISC.

7. It has or will adopt or change to one of the following tax years.

a. A tax year ending December 31.

b. A natural business year.

c. An ownership tax year.

d. A tax year elected under section 444.

e. A 52-53-week tax year ending with reference to a year listed above.

f. Any other tax year (including a 52-53-week tax year) for which the corporation establishes a business purpose.

For details on making a section 444 election or requesting a natural business, ownership, or other business purpose tax year, see Part II of Form 2553.

8. Each shareholder consents as explained in the instructions for column K.

See sections 1361, 1362, and 1378, and their related regulations for additional information on the above tests.

A parent S corporation can elect to treat an eligible wholly-owned subsidiary as a qualified subchapter S subsidiary. If the election is made, the subsidiary's assets, liabilities, and items of income, deduction, and credit are treated as those of the parent. For details, see Form 8869, Qualified Subchapter S Subsidiary Election.

When To Make the Election

Complete and file Form 2553 (a) at any time before the 16th day of the 3rd month of the tax year the election is to take effect, or (b) at any time during the tax year preceding the tax year it is to take effect. An election made no later than 2 months and 15 days after the beginning of a tax year that is less than 2½ months long is treated as timely made for that tax year.

An election made after the 15th day of the 3rd month but before the end of the tax year generally is effective for the next tax year. However, an election made after the 15th day of the 3rd month will be accepted as timely filed if the corporation can show that the failure to file on time was due to reasonable cause.

To request relief for a late election, the corporation generally must request a private letter ruling and pay a user fee in accordance with Rev. Proc. 2005-1, 2005-1 I.R.B. 1 (or its successor). However, the ruling and user fee requirements may not apply if the following revenue procedures apply.

● If an entity eligible to elect to be treated as a corporation (a) failed to timely file Form 2553, and (b) has

not elected to be treated as a corporation, see Rev. Proc. 2004-48, 2004-32 I.R.B. 172.
• If a corporation failed to timely file Form 2553, see Rev. Proc. 2003-43, 2003-23 I.R.B. 998.
• If Form 1120S was filed without an S corporation election and neither the corporation nor any shareholder was notified by the IRS of any problem with the S corporation status within 6 months after the return was timely filed, see Rev. Proc. 97-48, 1997-43 I.R.B. 19.

Where To File

Send the original election (no photocopies) or fax it to the Internal Revenue Service Center listed below. If the corporation files this election by fax, keep the original Form 2553 with the corporation's permanent records.

If the corporation's principal business, office, or agency is located in:	Use the following Internal Revenue Service Center address or fax number:
Connecticut, Delaware, District of Columbia, Illinois, Indiana, Kentucky, Maine, Maryland, Massachusetts, Michigan, New Hampshire, New Jersey, New York, North Carolina, Ohio, Pennsylvania, Rhode Island, South Carolina, Vermont, Virginia, West Virginia, Wisconsin	Cincinnati, OH 45999 Fax: (859) 669-5748
Alabama, Alaska, Arizona, Arkansas, California, Colorado, Florida, Georgia, Hawaii, Idaho, Iowa, Kansas, Louisiana, Minnesota, Mississippi, Missouri, Montana, Nebraska, Nevada, New Mexico, North Dakota, Oklahoma, Oregon, South Dakota, Tennessee, Texas, Utah, Washington, Wyoming	Ogden, UT 84201 Fax: (801) 620-7116

Acceptance or Nonacceptance of Election

The service center will notify the corporation if its election is accepted and when it will take effect. The corporation will also be notified if its election is not accepted. The corporation should generally receive a determination on its election within 60 days after it has filed Form 2553. If box Q1 in Part II is checked, the corporation will receive a ruling letter from the IRS in Washington, DC, that either approves or denies the selected tax year. When box Q1 is checked, it will generally take an additional 90 days for the Form 2553 to be accepted.

Care should be exercised to ensure that the IRS receives the election. If the corporation is not notified of acceptance or nonacceptance of its election within 2 months of the date of filing (date faxed or mailed), or within 5 months if box Q1 is checked, take follow-up action by calling 1-800-829-4933.

If the IRS questions whether Form 2553 was filed, an acceptable proof of filing is (a) a certified or registered mail receipt (timely postmarked) from the U.S. Postal Service, or its equivalent from a designated private delivery service (see Notice 2004-83, 2004-52 I.R.B.

1030 (or its successor)); (b) Form 2553 with an accepted stamp; (c) Form 2553 with a stamped IRS received date; or (d) an IRS letter stating that Form 2553 has been accepted.

 Do not file Form 1120S for any tax year before the year the election takes effect. If the corporation is now required to file Form 1120, U.S. Corporation Income Tax Return, or any other applicable tax return, continue filing it until the election takes effect.

End of Election

Once the election is made, it stays in effect until it is terminated. IRS consent generally is required for another election by the corporation (or a successor corporation) on Form 2553 for any tax year before the 5th tax year after the first tax year in which the termination took effect. See Regulations section 1.1362-5 for details.

Specific Instructions

Part I

Name and Address

Enter the corporation's true name as stated in the corporate charter or other legal document creating it. If the corporation's mailing address is the same as someone else's, such as a shareholder's, enter "c/o" and this person's name following the name of the corporation. Include the suite, room, or other unit number after the street address. If the Post Office does not deliver to the street address and the corporation has a P.O. box, show the box number instead of the street address. If the corporation changed its name or address after applying for its employer identification number, be sure to check the box in item D of Part I.

Item A. Employer Identification Number (EIN)

Enter the corporation's EIN. If the corporation does not have an EIN, it must apply for one. An EIN can be applied for:
• Online—Click on the EIN link at *www.irs.gov/businesses/small*. The EIN is issued immediately once the application information is validated.
• By telephone at 1-800-829-4933 from 7:00 a.m. to 10:00 p.m. in the corporation's local time zone.
• By mailing or faxing Form SS-4, Application for Employer Identification Number.

If the corporation has not received its EIN by the time the return is due, enter "Applied for" in the space for the EIN. For more details, see Pub. 583.

Item E. Effective Date of Election

 Form 2553 generally must be filed no later than 2 months and 15 days after the date entered for item E. For details and exceptions, see When To Make the Election *on page 1.*

A corporation (or entity eligible to elect to be treated as a corporation) making the election effective for its first tax year in existence should enter the earliest of the following dates: (a) the date the corporation (entity) first had shareholders (owners), (b) the date the corporation entity) first had assets, or (c) the date the corporation (entity) began doing business. This same date will be entered for item H.

A corporation (entity) not making the election for its first tax year in existence that is keeping its current tax year should enter the beginning date of the first tax year for which it wants the election to be effective.

A corporation (entity) not making the election for its first tax year in existence that is changing its tax year and wants to be an S corporation for the short tax year needed to switch tax years should enter the beginning date of the short tax year. If the corporation (entity) does not want to be an S corporation for this short tax year, it should enter the beginning date of the tax year following this short tax year and file Form 1128, Application To Adopt, Change, or Retain a Tax Year. If this change qualifies as an automatic approval request (Form 1128, Part II), file Form 1128 as an attachment to Form 2553. If this change qualifies as a ruling request (Form 1128, Part II), file Form 1128 separately. If filing Form 1128, enter "Form 1128" on the dotted line to the left of the entry space for item E.

Column K. Shareholders' Consent Statement

For an election filed before the effective date entered for item E, only shareholders who own stock on the day the election is made need to consent to the election.

For an election filed on or after the effective date entered for item E, all shareholders or former shareholders who owned stock at any time during the period beginning on the effective date entered for item E and ending on the day the election is made must consent to the election.

If the corporation filed a timely election, but one or more shareholders did not file a timely consent, see Regulations section 1.1362-6(b)(3)(iii). If the shareholder was a community property spouse who was a shareholder solely because of a state community property law, see Rev. Proc. 2004-35, 2004-23 I.R.B. 1029.

Each shareholder consents by signing and dating either in column K or on a separate consent statement. The following special rules apply in determining who must sign.
• If a husband and wife have a community interest in the stock or in the income from it, both must consent.
• Each tenant in common, joint tenant, and tenant by the entirety must consent.
• A minor's consent is made by the minor, legal representative of the minor, or a natural or adoptive parent of the minor if no legal representative has been appointed.
• The consent of an estate is made by the executor or administrator.
• The consent of an electing small business trust (ESBT) is made by the trustee and, if a grantor trust, the deemed owner. See Regulations section 1.1362-6(b)(2)(iv) for details.
• If the stock is owned by a qualified subchapter S trust (QSST), the deemed owner of the trust must consent.
• If the stock is owned by a trust (other than an ESBT or QSST), the person treated as the shareholder by section 1361(c)(2)(B) must consent.

Continuation sheet or separate consent statement. If you need a continuation sheet or use a separate

consent statement, attach it to Form 2553. It must contain the name, address, and EIN of the corporation and the information requested in columns J through N of Part I.

Column L

Enter the number of shares of stock each shareholder owns on the date the election is filed and the date(s) the stock was acquired. Enter -0- for any former shareholders listed in column J. An entity without stock, such as a limited liability company (LLC), should enter the percentage of ownership and date(s) acquired.

Column M

Enter the social security number of each individual listed in column J. Enter the EIN of each estate, qualified trust, or exempt organization.

Column N

Enter the month and day that each shareholder's tax year ends. If a shareholder is changing his or her tax year, enter the tax year the shareholder is changing to, and attach an explanation indicating the present tax year and the basis for the change (for example, an automatic revenue procedure or a letter ruling request).

Signature

Form 2553 must be signed and dated by the president, vice president, treasurer, assistant treasurer, chief accounting officer, or any other corporate officer (such as tax officer) authorized to sign.

If Form 2553 is not signed, it will not be considered timely filed.

Part II

Complete Part II if you selected a tax year ending on any date other than December 31 (other than a 52-53-week tax year ending with reference to the month of December).

Note. Generally, the corporation cannot obtain automatic approval of a fiscal year under the natural business year (Box P1) or ownership tax year (Box P2) provisions if it is under examination, before an area office, or before a federal court with respect to any income tax issue and the annual accounting period is under consideration. For details, see section 4.02 of Rev. Proc. 2002-38, 2002-22 I.R.B. 1037.

Box P1

Attach a statement showing separately for each month the amount of gross receipts for the most recent 47 months. A corporation that does not have a 47-month period of gross receipts cannot automatically establish a natural business year.

Box Q1

For examples of an acceptable business purpose for requesting a fiscal tax year, see section 5.02 of Rev. Proc. 2002-39, 2002-22 I.R.B. 1046, and Rev. Rul. 87-57, 1987-2 C.B. 117.

Attach a statement showing the relevant facts and circumstances to establish a business purpose for the requested fiscal year. For details on what is sufficient to establish a business purpose, see section 5.02 of Rev. Proc. 2002-39.

If your business purpose is based on one of the natural business year tests provided in section 5.03 of

Rev. Proc. 2002-39, identify if you are using the 25% gross receipts, annual business cycle, or seasonal business test. For the 25% gross receipts test, provide a schedule showing the amount of gross receipts for each month for the most recent 47 months. For either the annual business cycle or seasonal business test, provide the gross receipts from sales and services (and inventory costs, if applicable) for each month of the short period, if any, and the three immediately preceding tax years. If the corporation has been in existence for less than three tax years, submit figures for the period of existence.

If you check box Q1, you will be charged a user fee of $1,500 ($625 if your gross income is less than $1 million) (subject to change — see Rev. Proc. 2005-1 or its successor). Do not pay the fee when filing Form 2553. The service center will send Form 2553 to the IRS in Washington, DC, who, in turn, will notify the corporation that the fee is due.

Box Q2

If the corporation makes a back-up section 444 election for which it is qualified, then the section 444 election will take effect in the event the business purpose request is not approved. In some cases, the tax year requested under the back-up section 444 election may be different than the tax year requested under business purpose. See Form 8716, Election To Have a Tax Year Other Than a Required Tax Year, for details on making a back-up section 444 election.

Boxes Q3 and R2

If the corporation is not qualified to make the section 444 election after making the item Q2 back-up section 444 election or indicating its intention to make the election in item R1, and therefore it later files a calendar year return, it should write "Section 444 Election Not Made" in the top left corner of the first calendar year Form 1120S it files.

Part III

In Part III, certain qualified subchapter S trusts (QSSTs) may make the QSST election required by section 1361(d)(2). Part III may be used to make the QSST election only if corporate stock has been transferred to the trust on or before the date on which the corporation makes its election to be an S corporation. However, a statement can be used instead of Part III to make the election. If there was an inadvertent failure to timely file a QSST election, see the relief provisions under Rev. Proc. 2003-43.

Note. Use Part III only if you make the election in Part I (that is, Form 2553 cannot be filed with only Part III completed).

The deemed owner of the QSST must also consent to the S corporation election in column K of Form 2553.

Paperwork Reduction Act Notice. We ask for the information on this form to carry out the Internal Revenue laws of the United States. You are required to give us the information. We need it to ensure that you are complying with these laws and to allow us to figure and collect the right amount of tax.

You are not required to provide the information requested on a form that is subject to the Paperwork Reduction Act unless the form displays a valid OMB control number. Books or records relating to a form or its instructions must be retained as long as their contents may become material in the administration of any Internal Revenue law. Generally, tax returns and return information are confidential, as required by section 6103.

The time needed to complete and file this form will depend on individual circumstances. The estimated average time is:

Recordkeeping	9 hr., 19 min.
Learning about the law or the form	3 hr., 9 min.
Preparing, copying, assembling, and sending the form to the IRS	4 hr., 38 min.

If you have comments concerning the accuracy of these time estimates or suggestions for making this form simpler, we would be happy to hear from you. You can write to Internal Revenue Service, Tax Products Coordinating Committee, SE:W:CAR:MP:T:T:SP, 1111 Constitution Ave. NW, IR-6406, Washington, DC 20224. Do not send the form to this address. Instead, see *Where To File* on page 2.

**Resolution
of**

_____

a _____ **Corporation**

RESOLVED that the corporation elects "S Corporation" status for tax purposes under the Internal Revenue Code, and that the officers of the corporation are directed to file IRS Form 2553 and to take any further action necessary for the corporation to qualify for S corporation status.

Shareholders' Consent

The undersigned shareholders being all of the shareholders of the above corporation, a _____ corporation hereby consent to the election of the corporation to obtain S corporation status

Name and Address of Shareholder	Shares Owned	Date Acquired
_____	_____	$_____
_____	_____	$_____
_____	_____	$_____

Date: _____

_____

_____

_____

_____

_____

This page intentionally blank.

WAIVER OF NOTICE OF THE ANNUAL MEETING OF
THE BOARD OF DIRECTORS OF

_____

The undersigned, being all the Directors of the Corporation, hereby agree and consent that an annual meeting of the Board of Directors of the Corporation be held on the _____ day of _____, 20_____ at _____ o'clock ____m at _____, and do hereby waive all notice whatsoever of such meeting and of any adjournment or adjournments thereof.

We do further agree and consent that any and all lawful business may be transacted at such meeting or at any adjournment or adjournments thereof as may be deemed advisable by the Directors present. Any business transacted at such meeting or at any adjournment or adjournments thereof shall be as valid and legal as if such meeting or adjourned meeting were held after notice.

Date: _____

_____
Director

_____
Director

_____
Director

_____
Director

This page intentionally blank.

MINUTES OF THE ANNUAL MEETING OF
THE BOARD OF DIRECTORS OF

_____

The annual meeting of the Board of Directors of the Corporation was held on the date and at the time and place set forth in the written waiver of notice signed by the directors, and attached to the minutes of this meeting.

The following were present, being all the directors of the Corporation:

_____   _____

_____   _____

The meeting was called to order and it was moved, seconded, and unanimously carried that _____ act as Chairman and that _____ act as Secretary.

The minutes of the last meeting of the Board of Directors, which was held on _____, 20___, were read and approved by the Board.

Upon motion duly made, seconded and carried, the following were elected officers for the following year and until their successors are elected and qualify:

President: _____

Vice President: _____

Secretary: _____

Treasurer: _____

There being no further business to come before the meeting, upon motion duly made, seconded, and unanimously carried, it was adjourned.

_____
                                Secretary

Directors:

_____

_____

_____

_____

This page intentionally blank.

WAIVER OF NOTICE OF THE ANNUAL MEETING OF
THE SHAREHOLDERS OF

_____

The undersigned, being all the shareholders of the Corporation, hereby agree and consent that an annual meeting of the shareholders of the Corporation be held on the _____ day of _____, 20_____ at _____ o'clock ____m at _____, and do hereby waive all notice whatsoever of such meeting and of any adjournment or adjournments thereof.

We do further agree and consent that any and all lawful business may be transacted at such meeting or at any adjournment or adjournments thereof. Any business transacted at such meeting or at any adjournment or adjournments thereof shall be as valid and legal as if such meeting or adjourned meeting were held after notice.

Date: _____

_____
Shareholder

_____
Shareholder

_____
Shareholder

_____
Shareholder

This page intentionally blank.

MINUTES OF THE ANNUAL MEETING OF
SHAREHOLDERS OF

_____

The annual meeting of Shareholders of the Corporation was held on the date and at the time and place set forth in the written waiver of notice signed by the shareholders, and attached to the minutes of this meeting.

There were present the following shareholders:

Shareholder   No. of Shares

_____   _____

_____   _____

_____   _____

_____   _____

The meeting was called to order and it was moved, seconded, and unanimously carried that _____ act as Chairman and that _____ act as Secretary.

A roll call was taken and the Chairman noted that all of the outstanding shares of the Corporation were represented in person or by proxy. Any proxies were attached to these minutes.

The minutes of the last meeting of the shareholders which was held on _____, 20_____ were read and approved by the shareholders.

Upon motion duly made, seconded, and carried, the following were elected directors for the following year:

_____   _____

_____   _____

There being no further business to come before the meeting, upon motion duly made, seconded, and unanimously carried, it was adjourned.

_____
                                                    Secretary

Shareholders:

_____

_____

_____

_____

This page intentionally blank.

WAIVER OF NOTICE OF SPECIAL MEETING OF
THE BOARD OF DIRECTORS OF

_____

The undersigned, being all the Directors of the Corporation, hereby agree and consent that a special meeting of the Board of Directors of the Corporation be held on the _____ day of _____, 20_____ at _____ o'clock _____m at _____, and do hereby waive all notice whatsoever of such meeting and of any adjournment or adjournments thereof.

The purpose of the meeting is:

We do further agree and consent that any and all lawful business may be transacted at such meeting or at any adjournment or adjournments thereof as may be deemed advisable by the Directors present. Any business transacted at such meeting or at any adjournment or adjournments thereof shall be as valid and legal as if such meeting or adjourned meeting were held after notice.

Date: _____

_____
Director

_____
Director

_____
Director

_____
Director

This page intentionally blank.

MINUTES OF SPECIAL MEETING OF
THE BOARD OF DIRECTORS OF

_____

A special meeting of the Board of Directors of the Corporation was held on the date and at the time and place set forth in the written waiver of notice signed by the directors, and attached to the minutes of this meeting.

The following were present, being all the directors of the Corporation:

_____   _____

_____   _____

The meeting was called to order and it was moved, seconded, and unanimously carried that _____ act as Chairman and that _____ act as Secretary.

The minutes of the last meeting of the Board of Directors which was held on _____, 20____ were read and approved by the Board.

Upon motion duly made, seconded, and carried, the following resolution was adopted:

There being no further business to come before the meeting, upon motion duly made, seconded, and unanimously carried, it was adjourned.

_____
Secretary

Directors:

_____

_____

_____

This page intentionally blank.

WAIVER OF NOTICE OF SPECIAL MEETING OF
THE SHAREHOLDERS OF

_____

The undersigned, being all the shareholders of the Corporation, hereby agree and consent that a special meeting of the shareholders of the Corporation be held on the _____ day of _____, 20_____ at _____ o'clock _____m at _____, and do hereby waive all notice whatsoever of such meeting and of any adjournment or adjournments thereof.

The purpose of the meeting is:

We do further agree and consent that any and all lawful business may be transacted at such meeting or at any adjournment or adjournments thereof. Any business transacted at such meeting or at any adjournment or adjournments thereof shall be as valid and legal as if such meeting or adjourned meeting were held after notice.

Date: _____

_____
Shareholder

_____
Shareholder

_____
Shareholder

_____
Shareholder

This page intentionally blank.

MINUTES OF SPECIAL MEETING OF
SHAREHOLDERS OF

_____

A special meeting of Shareholders of the Corporation was held on the date and at the time and place set forth in the written waiver of notice signed by the shareholders, and attached to the minutes of this meeting.

There were present the following shareholders:

Shareholder   No. of Shares

_____   _____

_____   _____

_____   _____

_____   _____

The meeting was called to order and it was moved, seconded, and unanimously carried that _____ act as Chairman and that _____ act as Secretary.

A roll call was taken and the Chairman noted that all of the outstanding shares of the Corporation were represented in person or by proxy. Any proxies were attached to these minutes.

The minutes of the last meeting of the shareholders which was held on _____, 20___ were read and approved by the shareholders.

Upon motion duly made, seconded, and carried, the following resolution was adopted:

There being no further business to come before the meeting, upon motion duly made, seconded, and unanimously carried, it was adjourned.

_____
                                         Secretary

Shareholders:

_____

_____

_____

_____

This page intentionally blank.

Change of Registered Agent and/or Registered Office

1. The name of the corporation is:

2. The street address of the current registered office is:

3. The new address of the registered office is to be:

4. The current registered agent is:

5. The new registered agent is:

6. The street address of the registered office and the street address of the business address of the registered agent are identical.

7. Such change was authorized by resolution duly adopted by the Board of Directors of the corporation or by an officer of the corporation so authorized by the board of directors.

_____
Secretary

Having been named as registered agent and to accept service of process for the above stated corporation at the place designated in this certificate, I hereby accept the appointment as registered agent and agree to act in this capacity. I further agree to comply with the provisions of all statutes relating to the proper and complete performance of my duties, and am familiar with and accept the obligations of my position as registered agent.

_____
Registered Agent

This page intentionally blank.

Stock Transfer Ledger

Certificates Issued

Transfer Shares

Cert. No.	No. of Shares	Date Acquired	Shareholder Name and Address	From Whom Transferred	Amount Paid	Date of Transfer	To Whom Transferred	Cert. No Surrendered	No. of Shares Transferred	Cert. No.

This page intentionally blank.

Certificate No. _____
No. of shares _____
Dated _____
Issued to: _____
_____
_____

☐ Original issue
Documentary stamp tax paid:
$ _____
(Attach stamps to this stub.)

☐ Transferred from:
_____
_____
Date: _____

Original Cert. No.	Original No. Shares	No. of Shares Transferred
_____	_____	_____

Received Cert. No. _____
No. of shares _____
New certificates issued:

Cert. No.	No. of Shares
_____	_____
_____	_____

Certificate No. _____
No. of shares _____
Dated _____
Issued to: _____
_____
_____

☐ Original issue
Documentary stamp tax paid:
$ _____
(Attach stamps to this stub.)

☐ Transferred from:
_____
_____
Date: _____

Original Cert. No.	Original No. Shares	No. of Shares Transferred
_____	_____	_____

Received Cert. No. _____
No. of shares _____
New certificates issued:

Cert. No.	No. of Shares
_____	_____
_____	_____

Certificate No. _____
No. of shares _____
Dated _____
Issued to: _____
_____
_____

☐ Original issue
Documentary stamp tax paid:
$ _____
(Attach stamps to this stub.)

☐ Transferred from:
_____
_____
Date: _____

Original Cert. No.	Original No. Shares	No. of Shares Transferred
_____	_____	_____

Received Cert. No. _____
No. of shares _____
New certificates issued:

Cert. No.	No. of Shares
_____	_____
_____	_____

This page intentionally blank.

Stub 1

Certificate No._____
No. of shares _____
Dated _____
Issued to: _____

☐ Original issue
Documentary stamp tax paid:
$_____
(Attach stamps to this stub.)

Received Cert. No._____
No. of shares _____
New certificates issued:
Cert. No.	No. of Shares
_____	_____
_____	_____

☐ Transferred from:
_____
Date: _____

Original Cert. No.	Original No. Shares	No. of Shares Transferred
_____	_____	_____

Stub 2

Certificate No._____
No. of shares _____
Dated _____
Issued to: _____

☐ Original issue
Documentary stamp tax paid:
$_____
(Attach stamps to this stub.)

Received Cert. No._____
No. of shares _____
New certificates issued:
Cert. No.	No. of Shares
_____	_____
_____	_____

☐ Transferred from:
_____
Date: _____

Original Cert. No.	Original No. Shares	No. of Shares Transferred
_____	_____	_____

Stub 3

Certificate No._____
No. of shares _____
Dated _____
Issued to: _____

☐ Original issue
Documentary stamp tax paid:
$_____
(Attach stamps to this stub.)

Received Cert. No._____
No. of shares _____
New certificates issued:
Cert. No.	No. of Shares
_____	_____
_____	_____

☐ Transferred from:
_____
Date: _____

Original Cert. No.	Original No. Shares	No. of Shares Transferred
_____	_____	_____

This page intentionally blank.

The shares represented by this certificate have not been registered under state or federal securities laws. Therefore, they may not be transferred until the corporation determines that such transfer will not adversely affect the exemptions relied upon.

Certificate No.

Shares

Organized under the laws of the State of _____

This certifies that _____ is the holder of record of _____ shares of _____ stock of

transferable only on the books of the corporation by the holder hereof in person or by Attorney upon surrender of this certificate properly endorsed.

In witness whereof, the said corporation has caused this certificate to be signed by its duly authorized officers and its corporate seal to be hereto affixed this _____ day of _____, _____.

For value received, _____ hereby sell, assign and transfer unto _____,
_____ shares represented by
this certificate and do hereby irrevocably constitute and appoint _____
attorney to transfer the said shares on the books of the corporation with full power of substitution in the premises.

Dated _____

_____

Witness:

_____

The shares represented by this certificate have not been registered under state or federal securities laws. Therefore, they may not be transferred until the corporation determines that such transfer will not adversely affect the exemptions relied upon.

Certificate No. _____

Shares _____

Organized under the laws of the State of _____

This certifies that _____ _is the holder of record of_

_____ _shares of_ _____ _stock of_

transferable only on the books of the corporation by the holder hereof in person or by Attorney upon surrender of this certificate properly endorsed.

In witness whereof, the said corporation has caused this certificate to be signed by its duly authorized officers and its corporate seal to be hereto affixed this _____ _day of_ _____ .

_____

For value received, _____ hereby sell, assign and transfer unto _____,
_____ shares represented by
this certificate and do hereby irrevocably constitute and appoint _____
attorney to transfer the said shares on the books of the corporation with full power of substitution in the premises.

Dated _____

_____

Witness:
_____

The shares represented by this certificate have not been registered under state or federal securities laws. Therefore, they may not be transferred until the corporation determines that such transfer will not adversely affect the exemptions relied upon.

Certificate No.

Shares

Organized under the laws of the State of _____

This certifies that _____ is the holder of record of

_____ shares of _____ stock of

transferable only on the books of the corporation by the holder hereof in person or by Attorney upon surrender of this certificate properly endorsed.

In witness whereof, the said corporation has caused this certificate to be signed by its duly authorized officers and its corporate seal to be hereto affixed this _____ day of _____ .

_____

For value received, _____ hereby sell, assign and transfer unto _____,
_____ shares represented by
this certificate and do hereby irrevocably constitute and appoint _____
attorney to transfer the said shares on the books of the corporation with full power of substitution in the premises.

Dated _____

_____

Witness:

_____

The shares represented by this certificate have not been registered under state or federal securities laws. Therefore, they may not be transferred until the corporation determines that such transfer will not adversely affect the exemptions relied upon.

Shares

Certificate No.

Organized under the laws of the State of _____

This certifies that _____ is the holder of record of

_____ shares of _____ stock of

transferable only on the books of the corporation by the holder hereof in
person or by Attorney upon surrender of this certificate properly endorsed.

In witness whereof, the said corporation has caused this certificate to be
signed by its duly authorized officers and its corporate seal to be hereto
affixed this _____ day of _____.

For value received, _____ hereby sell, assign and transfer unto _____,
_____ shares represented by
this certificate and do hereby irrevocably constitute and appoint _____
attorney to transfer the said shares on the books of the corporation with full power of substitution in the premises.

Dated _____

_____

Witness:

_____

The shares represented by this certificate have not been registered under state or federal securities laws. Therefore, they may not be transferred until the corporation determines that such transfer will not adversely affect the exemptions relied upon.

Shares

Certificate No.

Organized under the laws of the State of

This certifies that

_____ is the holder of record of

_____ shares of _____ stock of

transferable only on the books of the corporation by the holder hereof in person or by Attorney upon surrender of this certificate properly endorsed.

In witness whereof, the said corporation has caused this certificate to be signed by its duly authorized officers and its corporate seal to be hereto affixed this _____ day of _____.

For value received, _____ hereby sell, assign and transfer unto _____,
_____ *shares represented by*
this certificate and do hereby irrevocably constitute and appoint _____
attorney to transfer the said shares on the books of the corporation with full power of substitution in the premises.

Dated _____

_____

Witness:

_____

The shares represented by this certificate have not been registered under state or federal securities laws. Therefore, they may not be transferred until the corporation determines that such transfer will not adversely affect the exemptions relied upon.

Certificate No.

Shares

Organized under the laws of the State of

This certifies that _____ is the holder of record of

_____ shares of _____ stock of

transferable only on the books of the corporation by the holder hereof in person or by Attorney upon surrender of this certificate properly endorsed.

In witness whereof, the said corporation has caused this certificate to be signed by its duly authorized officers and its corporate seal to be hereto affixed this _____ day of _____.

For value received, _____ hereby sell, assign and transfer unto _____,
_____ shares represented by
this certificate and do hereby irrevocably constitute and appoint _____
attorney to transfer the said shares on the books of the corporation with full power of substitution in the premises.

Dated _____

                                                                    _____

Witness:
_____

The shares represented by this certificate have not been registered under state or federal securities laws. Therefore, they may not be transferred until the corporation determines that such transfer will not adversely affect the exemptions relied upon.

Shares

Certificate No.

Organized under the laws of the State of _____

This certifies that _____ is the holder of record of

_____ *shares of* _____ *stock of*

transferable only on the books of the corporation by the holder hereof in person or by Attorney upon surrender of this certificate properly endorsed.

In witness whereof, the said corporation has caused this certificate to be signed by its duly authorized officers and its corporate seal to be hereto affixed this _____ *day of* _____.

For value received, _____ hereby sell, assign and transfer unto _____,
_____ shares represented by
this certificate and do hereby irrevocably constitute and appoint _____
attorney to transfer the said shares on the books of the corporation with full power of substitution in the premises.

Dated _____

_____

Witness:
_____

SHAREHOLDER AGREEMENT

WHEREAS the undersigned shareholders are forming a Corporation and wish to protect their interests and those of the Corporation, in consideration of the mutual promises and conditions set out below, the parties agree as follows:

1. **Best Efforts.** Each shareholder agrees to devote his or her best efforts to the development of the Corporation. No shareholder shall participate in any enterprise which competes in any way with the activities of the Corporation.

2. **Right to Serve as Director or Officer.** Each shareholder shall, so long as he or she owns shares in the Corporation, have the right to serve as a director of the Corporation or to designate some responsible person to serve as his or her nominee.

The officers of the Corporation shall be the following shareholders, each of whom shall continue to serve as long as he owns shares:

President _____
Vice President _____
Treasurer _____
Secretary _____

Any officer or director who ceases to be a shareholder shall no longer be an officer or director upon the transfer of shares.

3. **Salary.** The Corporation shall employ the shareholders and pay salaries to them as follows:

Name of Shareholder and initial salary

_____ $_____
_____ $_____
_____ $_____

The salary received by any shareholder as an officer or employee or in any other function or for any other service shall serve as compensation for all services or functions the shareholder performs for the Corporation. The directors may increase or decrease the salaries from time to time, upon unanimous vote.

4. **Additional Shares.** The Corporation shall not, without consent of all of the shareholders, do any of the following: (a) issue additional shares of any class or any securities convertible into shares of any class; (b) merge or participate in a share exchange with any other Corporation; or (c) transfer all or substantially all of the assets of the Corporation for any consideration other than cash.

In the event the shareholders agree to issue additional shares or securities convertible into shares, then each of the shareholders shall have the right to purchase any such securities so offered at a future date in proportion to his then respective interest in the Corporation at the time of such offer.

5. **Transfer of Shares.** No shares shall be transferred in any manner or by any means except upon unanimous consent of the shareholders. If a proposed sale is not agreed to by unanimous consent, a shareholder may resign from his or her positions with the corporation and be bought out by the corporation as provided below.

6. **Buyout.** Upon the death, resignation, adjudication of incompetency, or bankruptcy by any shareholder, or the transfer, agreement to transfer, or attachment of any shares, the Corporation shall purchase all of the shares of the shareholder so affected at the value of shares described below. Payment by the corporation for such buyout shall be within thirty days of the determination of value and the transferring shareholder shall execute all documents necessary to transfer his or her shares.

7. **Value of Shares.** The parties agree that upon execution of this agreement the value of each share of stock is $_____. This value shall be reviewed and updated once each year and at any time that a sale of shares is contemplated. New value shall be set by a unanimous vote of the shareholders. If the shareholders cannot agree, then the corporation's accountant shall be asked to set a value. If any shareholder disagrees with the corporation's accountant's value, he or she may get the value of another accountant. If the two accountants cannot agree to an acceptable value, they shall choose a third accountant to set the final value.

8. **S Corporation Status.** If the Corporation is an S corporation and if it reasonably determines that any proposed transferee is not eligible as a shareholder of a Subchapter S Corporation or that such transfer would cause the Corporation to lose its qualification as a Subchapter S Corporation, then the Corporation may so notify the shareholder of that determination and thereby forbid the consummation of the transfer.

9. **Endorsement.** The certificates for shares of the Corporation shall be endorsed as follows: "The shares represented by this certificate are subject to and are transferable only on compliance with a Shareholders Agreement a copy of which is on file in the office of the Secretary of the Corporation."

10. **Formalities.** Whenever under this Agreement notice is required to be given, it shall be given in writing served in person or by certified or registered mail, return receipt requested, to the address of the shareholder listed in the stock ledger of the corporation, and it shall be deemed to have been given upon personal delivery or on the date notice is posted.

11. **Termination.** This Agreement shall terminate and all rights and obligations hereunder shall cease upon the happening of any one of the following events:

(a) The adjudication of the Corporation as bankrupt, the execution by it of any assignment for the benefit of creditors, or the appointment of a receiver for the Corporation.

(b) The voluntary or involuntary dissolution of the Corporation.

(c) By a written Agreement signed by all the shareholders to terminate this Agreement.

12. **Entire Agreement.** This Agreement embodies the entire representations, Agreements and conditions in relation to the subject matter hereof and no representations,

understandings or Agreements, oral or otherwise, in relation thereto exist between the parties except as herein expressly set forth. The Agreement may not be amended or terminated orally but only as expressly provided herein or by an instrument in writing duly executed by the parties hereto.

13. **Heirs and Assigns.** This Agreement and the various rights and obligations arising under it shall inure to the benefit of and be binding upon the parties hereto and their respective heirs, successors and assigns.

14. **Severability.** The invalidity or unenforceability of any term or provision of this Agreement or the non-application of such term or provision to any person or circumstance shall not impair or affect the remainder of this Agreement, and its application to other persons and circumstances and the remaining terms and provisions hereof shall not be invalidated but shall remain in full force and effect.

15. **Gender.** Whenever in this Agreement any pronoun is used in reference to any shareholder, purchaser or other person or entity, natural or otherwise, the singular shall include the plural, and the masculine shall include the feminine or the neuter, as required by context.

16. **Arbitration.** All disputes between shareholders or between the corporation and a shareholder shall be settled by arbitration and the parties hereto specifically waive they rights to bring action in any court, except to enforce an arbitration decision.

17. **Choice of Law.** This Agreement shall be governed by and construed in accordance with the laws of the State of _____.

IN WITNESS WHEREOF, the parties hereto have executed this Agreement the date and place first above mentioned.

_____ [Name of Corporation]

By: _____,
                 President

                         _____ Shareholder

                         _____ Shareholder

                         _____ Shareholder

                         _____ Shareholder

This page intentionally blank.

OFFICER/DIRECTOR RESIGNATION
FOR A CORPORATION

I, _____, hereby resign as _____

[Title]

of _____, _____ a corporation

[Name of Corporation]   [Document Number, if known]

organized under the laws of the State of _____.

_____

[Signature of Resigning Officer/Director]

Index

Florida, 24, 38, 50
forbidden words, 25
foreign corporation, 13, 15, 71

G

Georgia, 50
goods, 24, 25, 34, 75

H

Hawaii, 50

I

Idaho, 50
Illinois, 51
Inc., 23, 24, 26
income, 14, 15, 16, 17, 34, 37, 46, 48, 61
Incorporated, 10, 13, 15, 18, 26, 48, 70, 71
Indiana, 51
information return, 15
insurance, 6, 9, 11, 16, 17, 18, 25, 50, 51,
    52, 55, 56
Internal Revenue Code (IRC), 12, 36
Internal Revenue Service (IRS), 7, 16, 34,
    39, 41, 67
IRS Form 2553, 16, 34, 39, 41, 67
IRS Form SS-4, 34, 41, 67
Internet, 21, 22, 24, 29, 47
investment, 1, 6, 9, 18, 27, 30, 43, 44, 45,
    46
investors, 1, 43, 44, 45, 46, 47, 54, 73
Iowa, 51

J

joint, 37

K

Kansas, 51
Kentucky, 51

L

lawyers. *See attorneys*
lease, 14
Letter to the Secretary of State, 29
liabilities, 1, 5, 6, 7, 11, 19, 27, 28, 37, 60,
    69, 70, 71, 72, 73, 74
licenses, 7, 8, 25, 42, 67, 72
limited liability, 5, 11, 19, 69, 70, 71, 72
limited liability companies (LLCs), 11, 69,
    70, 71, 72
loans, 15, 38, 44, 59
losses, 9, 12, 15, 16, 37
Louisiana, 37, 51

M

Maine, 51
Maryland, 52
Massachusetts, 52
meetings, 7, 10, 31, 32, 33, 34, 35, 38, 39,
    40, 61, 62, 67, 72, 73
merger, 18, 32
Michigan, 52
Minnesota, 52
minority interest, 12, 29, 30, 31